BACK TO THE FUTURE WITH CIVIL WAR COMPUTER ARCHIVES

SHARPSBURG, Md. (AP) — Visitors to Civil War battlefields soon will be able to ask a computer if their ancestors were Yankees or Rebels.

The National Park Service has begun to make a computerized directory of all 3.5 million Civil War soldiers. Historians estimate that at least half of all Americans have ancestors who fought in the "War Between the States."

"It's going to change the way we look at the war. It's going to personalize the battles, the struggles that went on," said Rich Rambur, superintendent at Antietam National Battlefield, one of two places where the computerized directory will be tested starting in the fall.

The computers are expected to provide names, home states, regiments, soldiers' ranks and whether they fought for the North or South, said John Peterson of the park service's computer division in Washington.

The computers will provide brief information on the 7,000 Civil War regiments and units, and information on many of the 10,500 battles, skirmishes and engagements, he said.

"We're also going to be able to track where Civil War soldiers are buried at our 11 Civil War cemeteries within the park system," Peterson said.

Computers are to be installed at all 28 Civil War sites that the National Park Service operates in 21 states and the District of Columbia.

The recent PBS series on the war helped pushed the project forward.

The Genealogical Societies of Utah, affiliated with the Mormon Church, and the Federation of Geneological Societies intend to enter the names on computer. Otherwise, it would cost the government $4.5 million to hire a company to computerize all the names.

The Lower Naugatuck Valley

Pictorial Research by Dorothy Larson

"Partners in Progress" by Margaret DeMarino

Produced in cooperation with the Lower Naugatuck Valley
Chamber of Commerce

Windsor Publications, Inc.
Chatsworth, California

The Lower Naugatuck Valley

A RICH AND BEAUTIFUL PROSPECT

An Illustrated History by Neil Hogan

Windsor Publications, Inc.—History Book Division
Managing Editor: Karen Story
Design Director: Alexander E. D'Anca
Photo Director: Susan L. Wells
Executive Editor: Pamela Schroeder

Staff for *The Lower Naugatuck Valley: A Rich and Beautiful Prospect*
Manuscript Editor: Mary Jo Scharf
Photo Editor: Robin Sterling
Editor, Corporate Biographies: Melissa W. Patton
Production Editor, Corporate Biographies: Justin Scupine
Proofreader: Michael Moore
Customer Service Manager: Phyllis Feldman–Schroeder
Editorial Assistants: Elizabeth Anderson, Dominique Jones, Kim Kievman, Michael Nugwynne, Kathy B. Peyser, Theresa J. Solis
Publisher's Representative, Corporate Biographies: Hannah Dresser
Layout Artist, Editorial: Bonnie Felt
Layout Artist, Corporate Biographies: Bonnie Felt
Designer: Ellen Ifrah

Windsor Publications, Inc.
Elliot Martin, Chairman of the Board
James L. Fish III, Chief Operating Officer
Michele Sylvestro, Vice President/Sales–Marketing
Mac Buhler, Vice President/Sponsor Acquisitions

Library of Congress Cataloging–in–Publication Data:
    Hogan, Neil, 1936–
    The Lower Naugatuck Valley : a rich and beautiful
    prospect: an illustrated history / by Neil Hogan.
    p.128 cm.22x28
    Includes bibliographical references and index.
    ISBN 0–89781–384–7
    Naugatuck River Valley (Conn.)—History. 2. Naugatuck
    River Valley (Conn.)—Description and travel—Views. 3.
    Naugatuck River Valley (Conn.)—Industries. I. DeMarino,
    Margaret. II. Lower Naugatuck Valley Chamber of
    Commerce. III. Title.
    F102.N2H64 1990 90–45676
    974.6'8—dc20 CIP

Contents

9 CHAPTER ONE
The Hill Southeast of Derby Landing

19 CHAPTER TWO
This Corner of the Wilderness

27 CHAPTER THREE
Turbulent Waters

37 CHAPTER FOUR
Deeds Not Words

47 CHAPTER FIVE
A New Epic

59 CHAPTER SIX
A Beauty Never To Be Forgotten

69 CHAPTER SEVEN
Some Things Old, Some Things New

87 CHAPTER EIGHT
Partners in Progress

123 *Bibliography*

125 *Index*

An Excursion Through Valley History

The battle between the USS Constitution *and the English frigate* Guerriere *is depicted in this dramatic painting by Michael Corne. One in a series of four paintings, this image shows the mizzenmast of the* Guerriere, *which was smashed by the assault from* Old Ironsides, *toppling into the sea. Commodore Isaac Hull of the* Constitution *reached the pinnacle of his career as a result of this confrontation—a victory that stirred the pride of the nation in the War of 1812. Courtesy, New Haven Colony Historical Society*

When the first train glided over the rails of the New Haven & Derby Railroad on August 5, 1871, it was packed with sightseeing New Haveners eager to get a look at the Lower Naugatuck Valley.

The next day the editor of the Derby newspaper couldn't resist poking a little fun at the city folks and crowing about the Valley and its people. "The sights of our place," he wrote, "evidently new to their provincial eyes, almost took their breath away . . . Our beautiful scenery, beautiful women, fine halls, large mills, crowds of people etc. being a common, everyday matter with us we thought little of it . . . "

Like that first journey on the Derby Railroad, it is hoped the excursion through this modest book will open the eyes of those so provincial as to be unfamiliar with the Valley and its communities—Derby, Shelton, Ansonia, Seymour, Oxford, and Beacon Falls—and will renew in those fortunate enough to live here an appreciation for its beauty and bustle.

The author's heartfelt thanks go first to those who, through the centuries, have made the Lower Naugatuck Valley a place that would take your breath away.

His thanks go also to those whose expertise and encouragement have made the excursion possible: Thomas P.Geyer, chief executive officer of the *New Haven Register*; Dorothy Larson of the Derby Historical Society; Lenn Zonder of *The Evening Sentinel* of Ansonia; Connecticut state archaeologist Nick Bellantonio; Judith Schiff of Yale University Archives; Barbara Costello and other members of the staff of the Connecticut State Library; Ann Kritemeyer of the New Haven Free Public Library; Jim Campbell of the New Haven Colony Historical Society; Karen Hallbach and Sally Hastings and the staff of the Derby Public Library; Bob Trella, Don Anderson, Mark Jaffe and Bob Barton of the *New Haven Register*; Angel Diggs and Wilbur Mesing, librarians at the *New Haven Register*; Romolo Tedeschi of the Lower Naugatuck Valley Chamber of Commerce; Richard Eigen, Kevin O'Mara, and Robert G. Frey, Jr., of the Valley Regional Planning Agency; Sue Kelley, Pam Schroeder, Jeffrey Reeves, and Mary Jo Scharf of Windsor Publications; Karen and Ryan Kieft; and, most of all, and as always, Tracey and Maureen.

*By the 1630s Dutch fur trading had established a firm
foothold in the New World, especially in the Housatonic
River area, where beaver was a popular trade item.
Within the next decade English settlers from the New
Haven Colony also became interested in forming their
own fur trade at Paugussett, a fact that the Dutch per-
ceived as an invasion of their rightful territory. Drawing by Claudia Farkas*

The Hill Southeast of Derby Landing

On Tuesday, September 17, 1811, one of New England's most famous early travelers, Timothy Dwight, left New Haven, Connecticut, to explore, as he put it, "those parts of the Housatonic which I had not hitherto examined, together with the whole length of the Hudson . . . "

Dwight's first stop along the way was the Lower Naugatuck Valley, just 10 miles northwest of New Haven. Arriving at the hill overlooking the town of Derby at the southern end of that valley, he paused, took pencil in hand, and jotted down his observations of the panorama stretched out before him in the splendor of an early autumn day in New England:

On the hill southeast of Derby landing there is a rich and beautiful prospect. The Housatonic, here a noble, navigable river, is in full view above and below for several miles . . . There is a beautiful island in its bosom. A considerable number of vessels are lying at the wharves on both shores . . . The houses and stores at Derby landing, and those at the Huntington landing, are sprightly, cheerful objects; and immediately above Derby, the Naugatuck, the largest tributary stream of the Housatonic, winding through chains of rich, verdant intervals, presents in its confluence with that river one of the finest ornaments of landscape. To complete the picture, several ranges of rude hills form a fine contrast to the soft scenery which I have mentioned and terminate the prospect on every side.

Timothy Dwight was not the first traveler to pause and gaze with an appreciative eye on the Lower Naugatuck Valley from this vantage point. Thousands of years ago—perhaps as early as 8600 B.C.—when the warming of the earth had melted the ice barrier that covered Connecticut, men first came this way. The sea level was then several hundred feet lower than now, and Long Island was still part of the mainland. Following the broad roadway of the Housatonic River northward in search of mastodon, mammoth, caribou, and elk, hunters eventually came to the hill overlooking the confluence of the Housatonic and Naugatuck rivers. Like Dwight, they too saw that it was a "rich and beautiful prospect," a place to linger.

These first Valley people were bands of hunters and gatherers, wandering along the rivers, camping for a season in natural rock shelters on the hillsides, and then moving on. As a testament to their presence in the Valley, they left only scattered implements of their way of life—stone tools, arrow points, fire sites, and the bones of the animals and fish they hunted.

At such a campsite in the hills of Oxford, archaeologists have discovered grooved axes, a grooved maul, and a quartz knife. Stone-lined graves, in which had been placed soapstone bowls, were found at a similar site in Shelton. And a rock shelter in Beacon Falls yielded a flint drill and flint arrow points, especially interesting because they suggest a trading network that included the Hudson River Valley in New York, the nearest place where flint is found.

As the centuries passed, temporary campsites gave way to permanent settlements, one of which was discovered just north of Indian Wells State Park on the west side of the Housatonic in Shelton. What researchers found there in the summer of 1936 tells much of the life-style of the Native Americans who called the Lower Naugatuck Valley home before the arrival of the Europeans.

Situated on a 300-foot-high ridge, running north and south, the Shelton settlement occupied a 10-acre site high above the

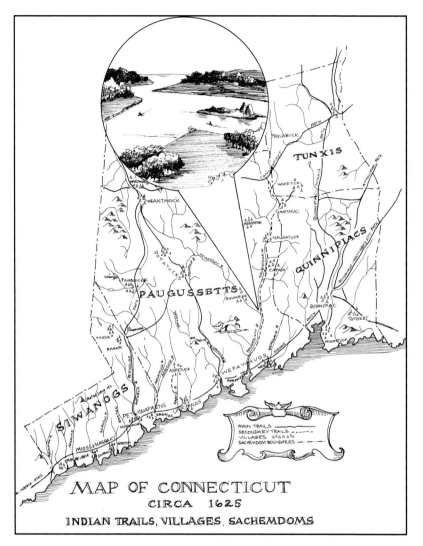

MAP OF CONNECTICUT
CIRCA 1625
INDIAN TRAILS, VILLAGES, SACHEMDOMS

The fertile Lower Naugatuck Valley, which famous New England traveler Timothy Dwight described in glowing terms in 1811, was a key intersection in the days of the Paugussett sachemdom. Not only were the rivers main travel routes for the Paugussett, the land trail running north and south along the mighty Naugatuck River connected the Lower Naugatuck Valley to the larger network of Native American trails. Drawing by Claudia Farkas

Housatonic. It was surrounded on all sides by heavy forest, and on its western slope was a spring where pure, cool water gurgled from a rock crevice into a stone catch basin constructed by the villagers.

In the center of the site were 200 fire-pits arranged in long, straight rows about five feet apart and facing on all sides onto an open square that apparently served—not unlike the village greens of the New England we know—as a common for meetings, ceremonies, and games.

The families that inhabited this sizable and commodious village above the Housatonic River were of the Algonquian people, the Eastern Woodlands Indians. The first Europeans knew them by several names. A Dutch

map of 1642 shows an Indian tribe named the Quirepeys astride the Housatonic River; while the English came to know the natives of this region as the Wepawaugs, Cupheags, Potatucks, and Paugussetts or Pagasucks.

The names are derived mostly from place names. Paugussett—modern-day Derby—means a place where the waters widen out. Potatuck—the natives' name for the Housatonic River—signifies a river with falls. Wepawaug—modern Milford—designates a land at the narrows of a river or cove. Cupheag—modern Stratford—signifies a harbor.

Estimates of the number of these natives, who came to be known generally as the Paugussetts, vary greatly. One historian says the population of Indians along the lower Housatonic and Naugatuck rivers was but 400. Another claims that the Indian warriors living just in the Huntington section of Shelton numbered 300, which, if true, would indicate a total population in that district alone of probably three times that many.

Whatever the case, the Indians enjoyed a comfortable standard of living. They dwelt in quonset-shaped homes covered with bark or closely woven rushes to make dwellings that were impervious to rain or cold in the wettest or most frigid weather.

The Valley yielded an abundance of food. Corn, squash, and beans were grown in large fields cultivated by the women. One early English visitor to Connecticut commented on the maize that grew to six or eight feet in height near Long Island Sound. And in the autumn, the men went north and west along the rivers to hunt, living in temporary huts and trekking at times as far north as Massachusetts.

In the summer, the Lower Naugatuck Valley natives did what modern Connecticut people do—they went to the shore to spend the dog days enjoying the cool sea breezes and feasting on fish and oysters. They also collected large numbers of clams, which they boiled, dried in the sun, and then sold to Indians in the interior, who were only too happy to trade venison or pelts for this great seashore delicacy.

It is quite likely that natives enjoying the seashore in the summer of 1614 might have seen a strange ship, its white sails billowing in the breeze, approaching from the west and dropping anchor at the mouth of the Housatonic River.

The captain of that ship was a Dutchman, Adrian Block. He had sailed in company with four other ships to New Netherland the previous year to purchase furs from the Indians of the Hudson Valley. When his ship, the *Tiger,* burned at its dock in New Amsterdam, Block, undaunted, built a 16-ton yacht, christened it the *Onrust* (or Restless), and set out to explore the region to the east.

Sailing through Hell's Gate and out into Long Island Sound, Block navigated along the Connecticut shoreline until he came to the mouth of the Housatonic. He paused there long enough to record that the river was about "a bow shot wide," and to name it the River of Roodenberg, or Red Hills. Then he weighed anchor and sailed east, exploring the Connecticut River, which he ascended as far as Wethersfield, the Rhode Island coast, and Cape Cod.

The Indians basking in the summer sun at the mouth of the Housatonic could not have realized it, but the appearance of that strange ship, which first drew near and then sailed off to the east, was the beginning of the end of the life they and their forebears had known for centuries in the Lower Naugatuck Valley.

The Dutch wasted no time claiming and exploiting the territory that Adrian Block explored in the *Onrust.* Just as they had done along the Hudson River, Dutch fur traders fanned out into the interior of Connecticut. A trading post—the House of Hope—was established at the site of modern Hartford and the trade in pelts flourished. On a trip through the region in 1642, the Dutch traveler and historian Adrian Van der Donck referred to the Housatonic River— the river "to which the name of Red Hills has

been given"—with the comment: "Many beavers are taken here, since a demand for our goods has stimulated the naturally slothful savages." While the Dutch were building a fur trade in the Housatonic and Naugatuck valleys, the English also were developing an interest in western Connecticut.

In 1637, during the Pequot War, English soldiers pursuing Pequot Indians westward along Long Island Sound gave glowing accounts of the region, accounts which fell on attentive ears in Hartford and Boston.

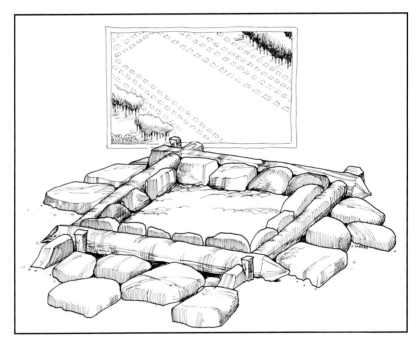

The very next year a band of Puritans under Theophilous Eaton and the Reverend John Davenport came from Boston to found New Haven at the place the natives called Quinnipiac. A year later some of these first New Haveners moved westward and founded Milford on the east bank of the Housatonic River. At the same time, a group of settlers from Hartford founded Stratford on the west bank of the same river.

One of the settlers at New Haven was a fellow named John Wakeman. In his native town of Bewdley, Worcestershire, England, Wakeman had been a timber merchant, and it wasn't long before he began to explore the hills and valleys around New Haven with an

The 200 firepits that were uncovered in the center of the Shelton settlement, located high above the west bank of the Housatonic River, indicate an advanced social organization unknown to the area's early rock shelter dwellers. The open square in the center of these firepits most likely served as a common area for ceremonies, tribal meetings, and games, not unlike today's charming New England village greens. Drawing by Claudia Farkas

Warm summertime months found the Paugussett women along the shore of Long Island Sound, where clams and fish were smoked and dried for consumption and future inland trade. Like the residents of today, these Lower Naugatuck Valley Indians traveled to the shoreline to enjoy the cool ocean breeze and to partake of the bountiful harvest of the sea. Drawing by Claudia Farkas

eye to timbering operations. He soon discovered a likely place at the confluence of the Housatonic and Naugatuck rivers—the place the Indians called Paugussett. There he set up operations and put some men to work felling trees.

The authorities at New Haven apparently felt the work being done in the Lower Naugatuck Valley was important, because in the spring of 1642—in the first reference to the place in the records of the English settlements—the General Court of New Haven Colony agreed to excuse two of Wakemen's employees from the mandatory guard duty "because of their imployment at Powgassett."

Several years later Wakeman—by now he had a couple of partners, Stephen Goodyear and Matthew Gilbert—touched off an international crisis when he built a small trading post at Paugussett with an eye toward doing some business with the natives.

Construction of the post brought a howl of protest from William Kieft, the Dutch governor at New Amsterdam. Kieft wasn't a very diplomatic fellow in the best of circumstances, and when Dutch traders came into New Amsterdam with reports of the new English post, he exploded.

In early August 1646 Kieft fired off a

letter to Governor Eaton of New Haven, accusing the New Haveners of having "an unsatiable desire of possessing that which is ours," and of having "entered the limits of New Netherland . . . not only to disturb our trade and to draw it to yourselves, but to utterly destroy it."

In his reply, Eaton conceded, "It is true we have lately upon Paugusset River, which falls into the sea in the midst of these English plantations, built a small house within our own limits, many miles, nay leagues from (Manhattan), from your trading house and from any part of Hudsons River." Eaton went on to admit the English purpose in building the house was to develop trade with the natives, but pointed out, in a sort of free-enterprise challenge to his Dutch counterpart, "We expect a little trade, but can compel none; the Indians being free to trade with you, us, Connecticut, Massachusetts or with any other . . . "

In September of that year, the representatives of the United Colonies of New England—New Haven, Connecticut, Massachusetts, and Plymouth—met in New Haven. Eaton gave a report on the troubles with the Dutch, pointing out that the New Haveners had not taken more than 20 beaver skins

from the trading house on the Paugussett.

For all his bluster, the Dutch governor was powerless to put a halt to what he considered virtually an invasion of New Netherland, and when he complained to the authorities back home, they merely cautioned him not to embroil the Netherlands in a war over the trading house on the Paugussett.

For their part, the English simply continued to do business in the Lower Naugatuck Valley. In addition to trading with the Indians, New Haveners began to cultivate crops in the Valley. New Haven records show, for example, that in November 1651 the son of John Benham was excused from a militia training day because he went "to Paugaset to cary a man some victualls which staid there ye Saboth to looke to the corne they were gathering and they had not victuals inough to leave him on the last day when they came home."

Nor were New Haveners the only English interested in the Valley. In the same year that Benham and his companions were growing corn there, a Milford resident, Edward Wooster, received permission from that town's authorities to grow hops for the brewing of beer at Paugussett. It appears that by 1652 Wooster and his brother-in-law, Edward Langdon, were already living at Paugussett, although actual settlement did not occur until 1654.

In fact, the Valley was fast becoming a haven for outlanders, those free spirits who like elbow room, and balk at the rules and regulations that go along with community life.

The matter of what to do about Paugussett was brought to a head in October 1655 when Richard Baldwin of Milford, rep-

resenting himself and nine others, went before the General Court in New Haven with a plan to buy up some land both from the Indians and from Wakeman and his partners in order to establish a town at Paugussett.

The partners—Edward Riggs, Edward Wooster, John Brown, Robert Denison, John Burwell, Samuel Hopkins, Thomas Langdon, Francis French, and Isaac Platt—were an assorted crew.

FAR LEFT: A typical Eastern Algonquin home was constructed with a strong sapling frame that was drawn together at the top, leaving an opening for the fireplace smoke to escape. The frame was then covered with thatch, or bark as pictured here, and tightly woven or sewn together to create a dwelling that withstood the elements. The door covering most used was an animal hide, and evergreen root was a popular thread. Courtesy, Derby Historical Society

LEFT: The main staples of the Lower Naugatuck Valley Indian diet were corn, beans, and squash. Sometimes referred to as the three sisters, these crops were grown in large fields cultivated by the women of the tribe. The beans were planted so they would crawl up the cornstalk, and together these three staples also helped to provide good nutrition for the soil once the crops were harvested. Drawing by Claudia Farkas

from henceforward shall looke upon it as a part thereof."

With that seemingly settled, Baldwin and his partners went ahead and purchased, on the east side of the Naugatuck River, "a tract of land at a place called Paugasuck." They laid out their purchase in equal shares, with each partner getting 1-1/2 acres for a home lot, four acres of upland, and three acres of meadow, with the exception that Baldwin got two home lots, six acres of upland, and four and a half acres of meadow.

The establishment of Paugussett wasn't yet an accomplished fact, however, for the General Court's approval of the new town unleashed a storm of opposition from Milford.

After a long and heated debate in early 1656, the court was forced to reverse its earlier approval just to keep the peace. "There was not like to be a comfortable closing betwixt (Milford and Paugussett) if the planting of Paugasett went on as had been intended," the court concluded, adding that those residing at Paugussett should "resign their purchase to Milford and that the towne of Milford would accomodate those of their towne that did intend to sit downe at Paugasett with comfortable accomodations . . . "

Baldwin objected, pointing out that the very reason he and his partners wanted to settle at Paugussett was because Milford did not have any extra land to pass out. The argument was joined once more and became so heated that the court had to urge both parties to be peaceable about the matter. One of the people at Paugussett, Thomas Langdon, was particularly vehement in declaring his intention to remain there, causing the court to caution: "If all consent but him, and he prove troublesome, the court will take a course either to quiet or remove him."

Baldwin wasn't about to abandon his project, however, and a few months later he came back with a compromise that he hoped would enable the people at Paugussett and Milford to "joyne in a loving way."

The Paugussett settlers, he explained to the court, would agree to purchase only

The Dutch ship Onrust, *also known as the* Restless, *left New Netherland (New York) under the command of Captain Adrian Block in the summer of 1614 to explore the Connecticut shoreline. Block sailed to the mouth of the Housatonic, named it the River of Roodenberg, and continued his travels east to Cape Cod. For the natives of Connecticut this expedition marked the beginning of the end of life as they had known it for centuries. Drawing by Claudia Farkas*

Baldwin seems to have been a lawyer, and it has been suggested that he got his legal training in a London law office before leaving for America. Riggs was a veteran of the Pequot War, probably one of those who had first explored the region while chasing the Pequots westward in 1637. Wooster and Langdon had long had an interest in Paugussett and were already living there. Some of the partners apparently were in it merely for the investment possibilities. Burwell, for example, almost immediately sold his share, as did Samuel Hopkins.

The court, after deliberation, told Baldwin that it accepted "him and ye rest of that company and the place called Paugaset under the jurisdiction (of New Haven), and

The ample woods at the confluence of the Naugatuck and Housatonic rivers provided English timber merchant John Wakeman with excellent resources for a lumbering operation, as well as an efficient means of transport by water. Timber became the first business in Paugussett to be recorded by the General Court in New Haven. Drawing by Claudia Farkas

those lands "over Naugatuck River and not toward New Haven bounds and also above them northward up into the country."

Second, the people at Paugussett would bear "their equall share of men which shall be pressed to any publique service." Third, the people at Paugussett would agree to pay their share for the maintenance of the minister at Milford for as long as they continued to attend church there, to pay a share of the Milford magistrate's salary, and to pay for the upkeep of the Milford meetinghouse until such time as they built their own meetinghouse. Finally, they agreed that the General Court in New Haven would settle any further disputes between Paugussett and Milford.

These terms were acceptable to Milford, and the whole issue of Paugussett quieted down until 1659, when Edward Wooster complained to the court in New Haven that he didn't know who was going to pay him the bounty for killing seven wolves at Paugussett.

Neither Milford nor New Haven

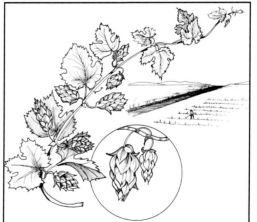

Edward Wooster received permission from Milford authorities in the early 1650s to grow hops at Paugussett. He chose the meadowland along the Naugatuck River in the area of present-day Ansonia/Derby Division Street for this new venture. Tradition holds that Wooster's irrigation ditches redirected the river from the west to the east side of the Valley. Drawing by Claudia Farkas

wanted to pay the bounty since Paugussett was not formally part of either town. Some delegates to the court pointed out that, whatever the status of Paugussett, the killing of the wolves benefited both Milford and New Haven. They urged that both towns "see what could be freely given him in recompense for his service."

The delegates, however, had about had their fill of the Paugussett problem. Since it

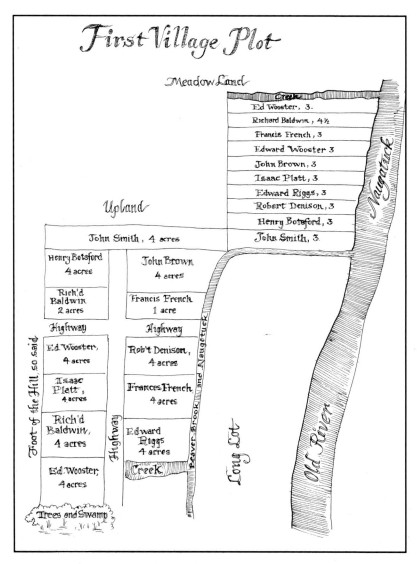

First Village Plot

Meadow Land

Ed Wooster, 3.
Richard Baldwin , 4½
Francis French , 3
Edward Wooster 3
John Brown, 3
Isaac Platt, 3
Edward Riggs, 3
Robert Denison, 3
Henry Botsford, 3
John Smith, 3.

Upland

Naugatuck

John Smith , 4 acres

Henry Botsford
4 acres

John Brown
4 acres

Rich'd
Baldwin
2 acres

Francis French
1 acre

Highway

Highway

Ed. Wooster,
4 acres

Rob't Denison,
4 acres

Foot of the Hill, so said

Isaac
Platt,
4 acres

Frances French
4 acres

Rich'd
Baldwin,
4 acres

Highway

Edward
Riggs
4 acres

Beaver Brook and Naugatuck

Long Lot

Old River

Ed. Wooster,
4 acres

Creek

Trees and Swamp

Representing himself and nine others, Richard Baldwin of Milford went before the General Court in New Haven in 1655 with a plan to establish a town at Paugussett. Having received permission for that purpose, the partners then laid out their land purchase in equal shares, dividing it into 1.5-acre home lots, 4-acre upland plots, and 3-acre meadowland plots. Drawing by Claudia Farkas

was obvious that Wooster and his cohorts were making precious little progress in organizing a town, the court "ordered that if the place called Paugasett become not a village to the purposes formerly exprest by ye court, betwixt this and ye general court in May next, that the place shall be deserted in reference to settled habitation."

The allotted time passed and Baldwin came before the court in May 1660 with the same old song and dance. An Indian, he said, had given him a tract called Hoggs Meadow, and he wanted the court to approve it as part of Paugussett. Yet, he had to admit that nothing more than putting up some additional fencing had been accom-

plished toward making Paugussett a town.

The court gave Baldwin a lecture, reminding him "that this matter of Paugasett had been four or five years under consideration and that the court had been often exercised with it and it was expected that they should have heard that Paugasett had been in a settled way to the ends pronounced before this time; but when the returns is given they only say they have done something about fencing and so it is delayed from court to court and held in a dallying way for four or five years together . . . "

Baldwin did what most of us do when confronted with our failure to meet a deadline. He fumed and fussed about delays that were not within his control, to which the court replied that it would give him one more year, "but if Paugasett become not a village by that time . . . and if the work goes not on in the meantime to the satisfaction of the court of magistrates in October next, Edward Wooster with any other that is there shall be removed and not suffered to live in such an unsatisfying way as now they doe."

While all this was happening, Stratford people also had been exploring northward. In 1659 Moses Wheeler, one of the first settlers at Stratford, bought from the natives some land in the White Hills along the Housatonic River across from Paugussett. Two years later another Stratford man, Joseph Judson, bought 5,000 acres there.

In 1663, New Haven Colony submitted to and became part of Connecticut Colony, and the nagging problems of Paugussett were turned over to the authorities at Hartford. They found them as vexing as had the New Haven authorities. In 1665, 1667, and 1669, the Connecticut court said it was ready to grant Paugussett the status of a town if the people there could pay for the upkeep of a minister, but nothing came of it.

Meanwhile, even without the formal status, the people at Paugussett were edging toward independence. As early as 1666 there is a record of the establishment of a general account out of which people were paid for

the Inhabetants of Pagasett that now are or shall be to the numbar of thirty: shall Pay to the purchesing of the minystores lott every man alike . . . " In November 1673, more specific plans were made for providing a home for the Reverend John Bowers, a Harvard graduate, who became the town's first minister.

With evidence of such splendid progress, the General Court of Connecticut finally, in May 1675, voted "upon the petition of Joseph Hawkins and John Hulls to have the privileges of a plantation granted to the inhabitants of Pagawsett there being about twelve families settled there already and more to the number of eleven preparing for settlement forthwith and that they have engaged a minister to come and settle amongst them speedily and have expended about 100 pounds in preparing a house for the minister . . . The plantation of Pawgussock is by this court named Derby . . . "

Thus, 50 years after the Dutch first explored the area, and 30 years after the English began to arrive, the Lower Naugatuck Valley finally had an official presence and name.

community services such as building fences. And on February 4, 1667, residents, in the first recorded town meeting, established policies governing the fencing in of their corn fields and the prevention of cows and swine getting into the common meadow.

And in a town meeting on April 11, 1672, the residents took the final necessary step to formal town status by voting "that all

LEFT: Until granted the status of a plantation, Paugussett settlers were obliged to attend church in Milford, to assist in the maintenance of the minister, and to help maintain the meetinghouse. It was an 11-mile trip on foot each Sunday to reach the meetinghouse, whose south view is depicted in this illustration that shows the building as it appeared in the mid-1600s. Courtesy, Derby Historical Society

BELOW: Although the plantation at Paugussett was having difficulty in attracting enough inhabitants to hire a minister, and thereby qualify for town status, it did report established policies governing the fencing of its corn fields and the prevention of cows and swine entering the common meadow in the first town meeting in 1667. Drawing by Claudia Farkas

Residents voted to build the community's first meeting-house in 1681, just eight years after the Reverend John Bowers had taken up residence in Derby. Probably constructed in the area along Prindle Avenue in Ansonia, between Pulaski Highway and Academy Hill, the building was completed in 1682 and served as the site for official town meetings, as well as for spiritual worship. Courtesy, Derby Historical Society

This Corner of the Wilderness

The English who settled the Lower Naugatuck Valley in the latter years of the seventeenth century had as keen an eye for utility as for beauty.

To be sure, the place they selected for their settlement was a scenic spot—"a panoramic amphitheater of beauty and perpetual joy," as one nostalgic Valley native, Albert Sherwood, called it two centuries later.

But the Lower Valley beckoned with more than quaint charm to colonists pushing outward from seacoast settlements.

In the 1600s water power was essential for commerce and for industry, and the site on which these hardy frontiersmen established Derby in the 1650s was the hub at which two of the colony's largest rivers met and flowed to the sea. To the northwest, the watery roadway of the 160-mile-long Housatonic River led all the way up into western Massachusetts. To the northeast, the Naugatuck River, from headwaters 40 miles away, flowed deep into the interior of Connecticut.

The two rivers met tidewater at Derby and from there cut a wide swath, 13 miles long, down to Long Island Sound, where there were abundant markets for crops, livestock, and manufactured goods. At this hub of Derby, the modern epoch of the Valley began to take shape from the very first years of the white man's settlement.

The year after the town was officially organized, a committee sent down by the General Assembly to view the lands at Derby found that lots were being laid out from the banks of the rivers, running up into the hills. Beside the river, the unforested meadows provided an abundance of marsh hay, adequate, if not ideal, fodder for livestock. Up from the river, on the hillsides, the woodlands were being cleared for crops and orchards, and fields were being fenced against the wanderings of livestock and wild animals.

A vote taken at a town meeting that same year shows even more clearly the economic forces that were coming to play in the Valley. On February 28, 1676, townspeople approved construction of a road, across land owned by Edward Wooster, down to the riverfront, "through the long lot and fishing place to the most convenient place to carry corn or other goods or land them there and a place at the water side of land sufficient to land in or set down any goods."

What was especially significant about the road was that it was not to be the usual narrow lane built in that era, so narrow that if wagons going in opposite directions met, one would have to pull off and wait for the other to pass. Instead, it was to be twice as wide as normal—in effect, the first superhighway in the Valley—"a sufficient cart way . . . for two carts to pass if need be one by another . . . "

The reason this superhighway was needed, of course, was that Derby was rapidly becoming what it would remain for more than a century—a regional market center. From the hills and valleys all around, farmers were beginning to bring their produce and livestock down to the riverside at Derby to be loaded onto ships and sent down the Housatonic for sale at nearby Milford, Stratford, and New Haven, or at more distant New York and Boston, and even as far away as the West Indies.

At first these farms were clustered about Derby landing, where the two great rivers met, but within a few years, the settlers were stretching out in all directions. In 1678 Samuel Riggs took up 20 acres near Rock Rimmon in modern-day Seymour, and by the early 1680s a number of settlers—Ebenezer Johnson, Abel Gunn, and Joseph

Early roads and bridges were the main transportation arteries in the Naugatuck Valley in the 1600s and 1700s, carrying both people and products throughout the region. Many of these early bridges, such as this one shown here circa 1870, were of king post design. An upright post was braced with side trusses, creating an inverted "V," which was repeated for the length of the bridge. Ferries, however, remained the only way to cross the Housatonic River until 1790. Courtesy, Derby Historical Society

Hawley among them—had staked out spreads in the Quaker Farms section of what is today Oxford.

Across the Housatonic River in the White Hills section of Stratford—modern-day Shelton—development was proceeding apace, although not without its territorial disputes. In 1678 Philip Denman and Daniel Collins of Derby leased some land in this region, but met with immediate opposition from Stratford because they had not been accepted as residents of that town.

Shortly thereafter Timothy Titharton came up from Stratford village and built a log cabin—the first home in the White Hills. Two years later Doctor Thomas Leavenworth bought one mile of land along the Housatonic near Indian Wells.

On both sides of the river, the silence of the primeval forest was shattered by the sound of axes felling trees, splitting them into logs for cabins (and later, salt box houses), rails for fences, and lumber for the basic tools used in agriculture—wooden plows, harrows, sickles, rakes, hoes, pitch-forks, flails, and winnowing baskets.

Before long, in the words of Jane DeForest Shelton, who wrote of her ancestral home in the White Hills, "Field after field lifted a smooth face to the bending skies, till the level hill-tops and sloping hill-sides were checkered with wheat and rye, with flax and barley, with corn and clover; and the barns grew wider and the coffers fuller, while the fulness of content reigned within the little house, as Nature's largess did without."

The construction of homes and the harvesting of grain, in turn, created the demand for mills. In 1676 Stratford gave James Blakeman permission "to sett up a sawmill at ye mouth of ye Farr Mill River," where that stream emptied into the Housatonic at the southern boundary of modern-day Shelton.

In August 1681 Derby townspeople—in an early example of offering incentives for industrial development—voted at a town meeting "to encourage such a man as will build a sufficient mill for the town of Derby, by giving him twenty pounds and build a dam . . ." John Hull took the town up on its offer and built Derby's first gristmill on Beaver Brook in what is now Ansonia.

In the early 1700s a new mill, built on the Naugatuck River in the vicinity of Pershing Drive, north of Division Street, known as the Old Yellow Mills, was being operated by Hull's grandson, Samuel, and had become a veritable industrial complex, complete with state-of-the-art technology. "For miles and miles the country round, even as far as Woodbury, Waterbury and New Haven," wrote Doctor A. Beardsley, "it was a central spot where farmers came with corn or rye in one end of the bag and a stone in the other, to get their grist ground . . . A set of stones were run day and night, which ground out monstrous quantities of linseed oil for exportation . . . An apparatus was so connected with some portion of the machinery, that after a given number of revolutions of the stones were made, a bell commenced ringing in a remote corner of the mills. This unseen signal told the story that the seed had run to oil . . . "

The rivers—teeming with shad, smelt, alewives, and eels—were no less prolific in those days than the land. On islands in the middle of the Housatonic, just below where it was joined by the Naugatuck, young boys spent their days catching roach, a small pan fish no larger than a human hand, while their fathers used seines and nets to haul in shad and alewives not by the hundreds, but by the hundreds of barrels.

Indeed, fishing was not just a pastime, but an industry from the earliest days of the settlement, Derby residents quickly discovering that the awarding of fishing rights could be a source of steady revenue for their town.

In May 1677 the town prevailed upon the General Assembly to grant to Derby residents "the benefit of the fishing trade to be to all and every of the inhabitants of Derby till the court shall order otherwise and do prohibit all others without their leave fishing within the bounds of their township."

The Derby residents followed up on this grant by declaring at town meeting: "If any that is not an inhabitant shall presume to fish without consent of the town in the bounds of the town he or they shall forfeit twenty shillings per barrel and so proportinately for all that he or they shall catch. . . "

For all this activity, however, the Valley remained a frontier settlement, bereft of amenities and exposed to isolation and danger. At one of their early town meetings, the residents themselves described it as "this corner of the wilderness," and when New England was engulfed by a war with the Indians, King Philip's War, in 1675, some Derby residents, at the suggestion of the General Assembly, removed "their best goods and their corn, what they can of it, with their wives and children, to some bigger town . . . "

Given such hardships, the population of the Valley grew slowly. Ten years after Derby was formally organized, there were only 38 persons residing there, and as late as 1709, the population had grown only to 49 persons.

To encourage homesteaders and discourage speculators and transients, the original settlers adopted a policy that four acres for a home, ten acres of upland, and four to six acres of meadow would be given to anyone who "shall build a sufficient house ac-

cording to the law and fence in his home lot and convenient outland and inhabit constantly for the space of four years . . . if they do not fulfill this order and shall go from the place and not fulfill these conditions shall forfeit all his and there grant of land . . . "

As much as they wanted their town to grow, however, the settlers did not want just anyone living at Derby. In fact, prospective residents were subjected to two town meeting votes: one granting or denying them permission to live there; the second granting or denying them the usual allowance of land.

And in at least one case, that of William Corsell, permission to live in Derby was denied. Corsell was reputed to be an infidel, and at a town meeting in August 1682, it was voted: "The town does not acknowl-

As early as 1678 Samuel Riggs was "granted liberty to take up twenty acres of land at or near Rock Rimmon on the west side of the river," in what is now modern-day Seymour. In that same year Ebenezer Johnson bought land from the Indians east and south of Rock Rimmon, settling on land that is the site of today's Oxford. To a society indoctrinated with the biblical word it is thought that the name Rimmon was a reference to Judges 20:45, "And they turned and fled toward the wilderness unto the rock of Rimmon." Courtesy, Charles Rotteck

edge William Corsell to be an inhabitant at Derby, and do desire the townsmen to warn the said Corsell out of town forthwith."

As harsh as that judgment seems today, it was in keeping with the code of these early Connecticut Puritans who believed that, like the chosen people of old, they had been led to this Promised Land and given the responsibility to build a society firmly rooted in biblical values.

In 1677 townspeople agreed at a town meeting that it was time "to gather a church at Derby and to walk in a church way and

RIGHT: From the early days of the Indians to the modern times of the twentieth century, the splashing waterfall known as Indian Well has been an attraction for all. Located about one mile north of the Housatonic Dam in Shelton, the Indians are said to have measured its depth at more than 100 feet, without finding its bottom. A quiet, romantic, and enchanting spot, Indian Well serves to soothe all who visit its natural beauty. Courtesy, Derby Public Library

BELOW: Of the 11 mills eventually set up along the Far Mill River in Shelton for sawing, grinding, cidermaking, and sorghum processing, this is the last one still standing. Now a private residence, it was previously known as the Eli N. Baldwin Stump Joint Factory (1865-1957), and was originally built as a woolen mill. The sickle-cut millstone standing at the building's edge once ground grain in a nearby mill dating from the colonial period. Courtesy, D.K. Jowdy

set up the ordinances of God according to gospel rules as near as we can attain according to our best light."

The small number of people in the community made it difficult to bear the expense and labor of constructing a meetinghouse, and it wasn't until November 1681— nine years after the Reverend John Bowers had taken up residence among them—that residents voted finally to build a place of worship.

Reverend Bowers died in 1687 and Derby was without a resident minister until 1694, when the Reverend John James accepted the offer of the town to provide him "forty pounds a year and the use of the parsonage and his fire wood."

James soon became a valued member of the community, serving not only as pastor of the church but also as town clerk and as the Valley's first teacher. James taught reading and writing to youngsters sent to him from December until April and received 40 shillings for his labors.

Across the Housatonic River in Ripton, settlers continued to travel to Stratford village to worship until 1717, when they complained to the General Assembly of the difficulty they experienced traveling eight or ten miles each Sunday and asked if they might not "have a minister among themselves at their own charges." The legislature

approved the petition and the settlers called the Reverend Jedidiah Mills, a 27-year-old Yale graduate from Windsor, Connecticut, to be their pastor, promising him "eighty pounds towards building his house, forty pounds of it in money and forty pounds of it in work, and in the beginning fifty pounds salary a year . . . "

A genealogy of the DeForest family of early Ripton contains a description of the Sunday routine of these settlers and says much about their staunch faith:

The ride from Moose Hill to Ripton meetinghouse was long, about four miles, though the number of miles could make no difference to the parishioners, since go they must . . . Such a journey was not unpleasant if the weather was good; there was always the possibility of meeting friends or neighbors and chatting as they jogged on together; there was so little time for visiting that early settlers eagerly seized this chance for sociability.

At last they would arrive at Ripton Centre, veritably a "centre," for families on horseback or on foot, if they came from nearby, could be seen gathering

from every direction and emerging on the Green. This was long and narrow, the meetinghouse standing on one end and the stocks and whipping post close at hand. Dismounting at the "Sabba'day House," a large building in the rear of the meetinghouse, the worshippers would, in winter, crowd around the brisk fire to get warm after their cold ride . . . The meetinghouse was a barrack-like building and bitter cold in winter . . . No wonder if the women in spite of their brief warming by the fire in the Sabba'day House drew their quilted hoods closer when they crossed the threshold of the sanctuary or if the children pulled up their mittens and mufflers . . . Nor could the sermons themselves have exerted other than a chilling influence if we may judge from the titles of those preached by the Rev. Mr. Mills, for instance, "An Inquiry concerning the state of the unregenerate under the Gospel. Whether on every rising degree of internal light conviction and amendment of life they are (while unregenerate) undoubtedly on the whole more vile, odious and abominable (in God's sight) than they would have been had they continued secure and at ease going on in their sins under the same external means of light."

Such Calvinistic theology was not to the liking of all the settlers; and before too many years, the Church of England began to make converts in the Valley, as in the entire colony. This set the stage for a confrontation because the Puritan faith was the established church by law and all residents were required to pay for its support.

Several of the Anglicans in Ripton Parish, Timothy Titharton and Daniel Shelton among them, refused to pay their share of the tax and were arrested in the middle of the night in December 1709, according to documents preserved in Connecticut Episcopal Church archives. The Anglicans were "forced to travel, under very bad circumstances, in the winter season, and at that unseasonable time of night, to the common gaol, where felons are confined, being eight miles distant, not allowing them so much as fire or candle light for their comfort and there continued them until they paid

such sums as by the gaoler demanded . . . " In Shelton's case, his captors "barbarously laid violent hands on his person and flung his body across a horse's back and called for ropes to tie him on the horse . . . "

Despite such intimidation, the Anglicans in Ripton Parish persisted in their faith, periodically seeking help from church authorities in London.

By 1734 Anglican missionaries were visiting the Valley regularly, and in 1737 John and Abigail Holbrook gave a plot of land in Derby for the construction of the first Anglican house of worship. The little congregation was served by the Reverend Jonathan Arnold, a missionary who lived in West Haven and traveled up the Valley as far as present-day Waterbury.

Other Anglican itinerants visited the faithful in Derby, one of them finding a decidedly cool reception because of his nationality. In a letter to church authorities, the

Wampanoag chief King Philip Metacom, son of the great chief Massasoit, determined that white settlement of southern New England be stopped. The ensuing King Philip's War (1675-1676) was perhaps the bloodiest of all seventeenth-century wars between American colonists and the Native Americans. Many local Naugatuck Valley residents were forced to seek shelter in the larger, more protected towns during the duration of this destructive conflict. Courtesy, New York Public Library

Shipping activity at Derby was a common sight by the early 1700s as the port rapidly developed into a regional market center. Grain, lumber, and livestock were shipped to the West Indies in return for rum, molasses, and exotic spices. Drawing by Claudia Farkas

Reverend James Lyons, a native of Ireland, complained:

As soon as they had advice of my appointment, and from what country I came and, indeed, before I arrived among them, they abused me, calling me an "Irish Teague and Foreigner," with many other reflections of an uncivilized and unchristian kind; they boasted they would either find or fasten something upon me relating to my character or conduct whereby they might get rid of me . . . It would be too tedious to record all the abuse and insults I have received at Derby; so many and so severe, that some of themselves, more moderate than the rest, remonstrated to them the danger they were in of losing the mission by their abuses to me . . .

Lyons was one of a handful of non-English people who turned up in the Valley in early colonial times. Among these "foreigners" were a few Huguenots, French Protestants who fled to the New World to escape persecution in Catholic France.

Indeed, Doctor John Durand, Derby's first physician, was of Huguenot stock. Born in La Rochelle, France, in 1664, Durand spent a year in South Carolina before coming to New Rochelle, New York, then to Milford where he married Elizabeth Bryant, daughter of the wealthy Milford merchant, Alexander Bryant. Durand settled in Derby about 1685. While he is referred to in colonial records as "chiurgeon," or surgeon, Durand was known to townspeople simply as "the little French doctor."

Several Jews also found a home in the Valley. One of them, Abraham Pinto, is listed on a Derby tax list of 1718 as having real estate valued at 29 pounds. Pinto owned land in Quaker Farms in what is now Oxford. Another Jew who immigrated to the Valley, Mordecai Marks, who was in Stratford in 1729, moved to Derby. His son in 1766 settled in Huntington in present-day Shelton, where he became a prosperous merchant. He died in 1797, leaving his trade to his sons.

African-Americans, too, were among the early Valley residents, although they came not as free men, but as slaves. Their presence is attested to by one 1738 Derby church record, which indicates that plans were made "to build a Convenient Seat for the Negros on ye beams over ye front Gallery and Stairs to go up . . ."

Native Americans were also kept as slaves, a fact that probably says more about the true relationship of the original inhabitants and the settlers than the many land deeds that appear in the history books.

One interesting case of Native American slavery is that of a girl named Dinah, who was the subject of a deed drawn up on June 8, 1722:

Know all men by these presents, that I, Joseph Gorham of Stratford, in the county of Fairfield, in the colony of Connecticut, for and in consideration of sixty pound money in hand received and well and truly paid by Col. Ebenezer Johnson of Derby, in the county of New Haven and colony aforesaid, to my full satisfaction and content, have sold and made over to the said Ebenezer Johnson and to his heirs, executors and assigns forever, one Indian woman, named Dinah, of about twenty-six years of age, for him, the said Johnson, his heirs, executors and assigns, to have, hold and enjoy the said Indian woman Dinah as his and their own proper estate from henceforth forever during the said Dinah's life . . .

When the colonel died, his widow passed Dinah along in another deed which stated, "for the parental love and good-will . . . and for divers other good and well-advised considerations . . . have given and do by these presents fully, freely and absolutely give, grant and confirm unto my beloved son, Timothy Johnson, him, his heirs and assigns forever . . . one Indian woman called Dinah and also a feather bed."

Colonel Johnson did a lot of trafficking in Native Americans. In one instance, he sold a female slave, Sarah, to an Indian named Chetrenasut, who wished to marry her. Chetrenasut won his bride's freedom from the colonel for 3 pounds, 10 shillings, and a tract of land known as Nayumps, located in modern-day Beacon Falls.

In another instance, Johnson freed an Indian slave named Toby, whom he had purchased in New London years before. After his manumission, Toby acquired from other Indians, for 10 pounds and a barrel of cider, a mountainous tract in the northwestern part of Beacon Falls. The land, which rises 500 feet above the western bank of the Naugatuck River, came to be known as Toby's Rock. The Native American ownership of Toby's Rock was short-lived, however, for after Toby's death in 1734, it

1734, it passed to Colonel Johnson's sons.

Given such experiences with the white settlers, the Native American population of the area dwindled rapidly during the late 1600s and early 1700s. Those Native Americans who escaped the scourges of such diseases as smallpox tended to emigrate northward along the Housatonic and Naugatuck rivers, away from the white settlements.

In 1761 Ezra Stiles of Yale reported that he had been told that "by Derby Ferry there were 50 years ago about eight or 10 wigwams, probably containing 10 to 12 families, but now no remains of them. At Turkey Hill at the lower corner of Derby, by the river, there was an Indian village of I suppose eight or 10 families, who had a tract of land secured to them by the government; they have continued the longest of any, but they are now reduced to but one or two broken families . . . "

For both white man and red man, change is the inevitable rule of human life, and even as Stiles was noting the passing of the Native Americans from the stage of Valley history, winds of change were beginning to stir that would soon sweep away the simple Puritan farming society that had put its mark on the Valley during the late 1600s and early 1700s.

The Puritan Church in the late 1600s and early 1700s was the established church of the Connecticut colony by law, and all residents were required to pay for its support. Disagreements arose in the Ripton Parish, however, when the Church of England began to make converts in the Lower Naugatuck Valley. Religious disputes continued for many years, and it wasn't until 1818 that church and state were separated in Connecticut. This 1846 illustration on the Huntington Green depicts the Congregational Church on the left, with the Anglican Church on the right. Courtesy, Charles Rotteck

Revolutionary War hero Lieutenant Colonel David Humphreys of Derby is portrayed in this oil painting by an unknown artist, delivering the standards of the defeated British army to the assembled Continental Congress in Philadelphia. Appointed as aide and secretary to General George Washington during the war, Humphreys was selected to receive the enemy's colors when General Cornwallis surrendered following the battle at Yorktown, Virginia, in 1781. Although the war did not officially conclude until the Peace Treaty of 1783, American independence was essentially won in this decisive confrontation. The selection of Humphreys for this important task illustrated the high regard and ability that Washington had placed in his trusted aide-de-camp. Courtesy, New Haven Colony Historical Society

Turbulent Waters

In the autumn of 1740 the magnificent hills of the Lower Naugatuck Valley were aflame with the spirit of born-again Christianity as well as the splendor of autumn leaves.

A series of revivals in the Connecticut River Valley in the late 1730s had blossomed into a full-fledged religious awakening—the Great Awakening, as it was ever after called—and the ardor of that awakening was sweeping through the colony, leaving in its wake a trail of repentance and conversion.

In truth, the Great Awakening was like a watershed in Connecticut and Lower Naugatuck Valley history. Behind it lay 100 years of slow, quiet growth, a time of planting and nurturing this corner of the wilderness. Ahead of it lay turbulent waters, a half-century of rapid and profound change that would reshape a narrow Puritan theocracy into a pluralistic and democratic society and replace colonial status with national independence.

The Great Awakening itself shook the colony's institutions and provoked its first significant religious and political disputes. Welcomed by the "New Lights," those who longed for emotion and personal involvement in religion and welcomed change, the Great Awakening alarmed the "Old Lights," those who saw its excesses as a threat to the venerable institutions of this land of steady habits.

Throughout the colony, these two forces—the liberals and conservatives of that age—clashed on the issues raised by the Great Awakening—freedom of religion, church-state relations, control by the people of their institutions. Nowhere were the confrontations more intense than in the Lower Naugatuck Valley.

The famous English missionary George Whitefield was preaching across Connecticut that autumn and he was enthusiastically greeted by the Reverend Jedidiah Mills, the ardent New Light pastor of the church in Ripton, modern-day Shelton. "Was refreshed this morning," Whitefield wrote in his journal when Mills came to hear him preach in New Haven, "by the sight of Mr. Jedidiah Mills, the minister at Ripton near Stratford. He wrote to me some time ago. I felt his letter and now also felt the man. I could not help thinking God would do great things by him. He had a remarkable work in his parish some time ago, and talked like one who was no novice in Divine things . . . "

Mills returned to Ripton even more fired up than usual with religious fervor, and the message he spread among his parishioners soon bore fruit in marvelous manifestations of God's grace. Sinners repented, those who had fallen away returned to worship, and people were filled with love for the church.

All these things were not to the liking of the Old Lights, however, and the next spring, when the Reverend James Davenport, a truly wild-eyed revivalist, came up to Ripton from Long Island to rekindle the flames, the Old Lights laid a trap for him and his host, Reverend Mills.

Over the winter, the Old Lights had used their majority in the General Assembly to pass a law designed to rein in the itinerant preachers who wandered the countryside stirring up the faithful. The law provided, among other things, that non-Connecticut clergymen could not come into the colony and preach.

The Old Lights chose to make Davenport's appearance in Ripton the first test case for that new law. Two of them, Captain Joseph Blacklatch and Samuel Adams, journeyed up to Hartford on May 29, 1741, and

filed a formal complaint charging that Davenport and his companion, the Reverend Benjamin Pomeroy, had arrived in Ripton on May 19 and "with certain illiterate persons . . . were collecting assemblies of people, mostly children and youth, and under pretense of religious exercises were inflaming them with a bad spirit and with doctrines subversive of all law and order; by which the peace of the town was greatly disturbed."

The legislature issued a warrant and Davenport and Pomeroy were seized at Ripton, hauled before the legislators in Hartford, and tried for preaching without permission. The trial was a raucous one. Davenport's supporters—some of them undoubtedly from Ripton Parish—threatened to overpower the sheriffs and spirit the two preachers away. They were prevented from doing so only by the calling out of the militia. After two days of deliberations, Pomeroy was freed, but Davenport was ordered out of the colony. Not trusted to leave of his own accord, he was escorted down to the riverfront at Hartford and put on a boat headed for Long Island.

New Lights throughout Connecticut were outraged by this heavy-handed violation of what they considered their civil rights, and people like Jedidiah Mills quickly showed that they would not be intimidated by the law-and-order faction. As if to flout the law against itinerancy, which the New Lights saw as a return to the very church-state repression that had caused their Puritan forefathers to flee England, Mills rode down to Stratfield Parish—modern-day Bridgeport—in June 1742 and began preaching revivalism to the people.

The justice of the peace at Stratfield filed a complaint against Mills, and the authorities promptly cut off the preacher's salary, preventing him from receiving the money due him from taxes collected in Ripton. So serious was the rift that the hold on Mills' salary was not lifted until seven years later, when the General Assembly finally approved a petition to return Mills to full grace.

Across the Housatonic River in Derby, where another confirmed New Light, the Reverend Daniel Humphreys, was pastor, the

Great Awakening left its mark, too. Like Mills, Humphreys considered the law against itinerant preaching to be the government's unconscionable meddling with the people's right to worship as they pleased. Like Mills, too, Humphreys openly violated the law by preaching to a Baptist congregation in New Haven in 1742. That indiscretion earned him the censure of the New Haven County ministers' association. Unrepentant, the Derby pastor exacerbated the situation two years later by participating in the ordination of a New Light minister, the Reverend Jonathan Lee in Salisbury. The New Haven County ministers wasted no time in suspending Humphreys a second time.

Having made their small but important contributions to freedom of religion in Connecticut, Humphreys and Mills moved offstage as even more unsettling events—events originating in the drama of international affairs—began to touch the life of the Lower Naugatuck Valley.

In 1744, for the first time since 1713, war broke out between the English and French in North America. It was the beginning of almost 20 years of intermittent hostilities—King George's War from 1744 to 1748, the French and Indian War from 1754 to 1760. And the stakes were high: control of a continent.

The human and material resources of the Valley were stretched by the struggle. Farmers found ready markets for their goods, and some merchants prospered supplying provisions to the army. But their good fortune was offset by the tears of mothers and wives who watched sons and husbands march off to face death in distant places with strange names like Louisburg, Crown Point, Oswego, and Quebec.

In some cases, military service meant only a few days of uneventful service guarding the frontier; but in others, it meant long-term commitments, and fame and fortune.

David Wooster, whose family lived at various times both in Derby and in the Rip-

ton section of Shelton, rose through the ranks to become a colonel commanding a brigade of colonial troops. In 1745 Wooster was a captain in the regiment of Colonel Aaron Burr in the expedition against the French fortress of Louisburg in Nova Scotia. He commanded the colonial ship *Connecticut*, which ferried troops to Cape Breton where the fortress was located. His service won him an appointment as one of the American officers on a ship taking prisoners to Europe. While in England, he was presented to the king and accepted a commission in the regular army.

Peter Wooster, of the Oxford section of Derby, was less fortunate than his kinsman.

Wives of the men who had been called to fight in order to protect British interests in the colonies in the mid-1700s not only struggled in the daily operation of their households, but were also burdened with constant concern for their husbands' safety. Shipwrecks, disease, and other unexpected tragedies of war called forth their deepest faith to see them through. Courtesy, Derby Historical Society

Grandson of Derby's first settler, General David Wooster was born in 1710 in the Far Mill section of Huntington, where his parents owned several hundred acres of land. Completely devoted to the interests of his country, Wooster served as a captain under Colonel Aaron Burr in the expedition against the French fortress of Louisbourg in Nova Scotia and gave his life for his country during the American Revolution. Courtesy, Jeanette LaMacchia

Peter enlisted as a corporal in the 4th Connecticut Regiment at the outbreak of the French and Indian War in 1754 and climbed the ranks to become an ensign in 1758. On August 8 of that year, while serving in a company of rangers under the command of future Revolutionary War hero Israel Putnam, Wooster was involved in a skirmish with the French and Indians at Wood Creek on Lake Champlain. He suffered six wounds from musket fire; had his left elbow, wrist, and hand shattered by the blows of a hatchet; and received nine hatchet blows to the head. The enemy scalped and stripped him and left him for dead.

Carried from the battlefield by his comrades, Wooster recovered and, after returning to Connecticut, went before the General Assembly in March 1759 to complain that "his arms are so disabled as to be almost useless in the common labours of life &c." and to ask "this Assembly to make him such grant or allowance as they think just." The legislature responded by granting him 40 pounds out of the treasury, but Peter died the next year.

While nursing their own wounds from the conflict, Valley residents also witnessed firsthand some of the hardships suffered by

their enemies. In 1756 the British uprooted thousands of Acadians, French residents of Nova Scotia whose loyalty was suspect, and scattered them among the British colonies. Connecticut authorities spread the 406 Acadian families allocated to the colony among the various towns. Four families were assigned to Derby and 14 to Stratford, presumably some of the 14 to Ripton Parish in the Valley.

Eventually, many, if not all, of the Acadians returned to Nova Scotia, unlike another Frenchman who came to the Valley in 1759 as a prisoner of war and remained to become one of its most respected citizens. His name was Claude Bartheleme, and years later he wrote to his brother in France, telling of the strange odyssey that brought him to the Valley:

This is to inform you of my very humble respects and to inquire after the health of my friends. I am still in good health, thanks be to God. I should inform you that after quitting you to make a tour of France, I engaged in the Regiment Royal Rossilon in the year 1756. Some of us embarked for Canada. I continued in good health until we arrived on the bars of Newfoundland; there a malady broke out on board the vessel . . . In 1757, we went to besiege Fort George, which surrendered after a siege of nine days, when we made eighteen scores of savages see the expediency of surrendering . . . In 1758 we gained a victory over the English, who were ten thousand men strong, we having only three thousand men . . . In the year 1759, in the month of May, we set out for Niagara, near which 170 of us found a health-house . . . and after sustaining it for twenty days we were obliged to surrender. Afterwards we were brought to New England where I married a girl in 1762 by whom I had three children . . . I built me a house in which I dwelt and afterwards another log house, in which I lived as well, thank God. In the year 1762, I learned to read and write English . . .

The wars were also at the root of the Valley's first crime wave. To pay for the maintenance of troops, Connecticut in the 1740s began to issue large amounts of paper money. The temptation was too much for those who dreamed of getting rich quick, and it wasn't long before the Valley was home for one of the most notorious counterfeiting gangs of early American history.

The gang was exposed in the autumn of 1746, when Daniel Grant of Newtown became suspicious of a Connecticut 20-shilling bill passed to him. As he suspected, the bill proved to be bogus, and authorities quickly were able to trace it back to Samuel Weed of Derby. Constable Samuel Tomlinson and a couple deputies went to Weed's home, where they found plenty of evidence: a press, two bottles of red ink, a plate for making Rhode Island 40-shilling notes, and a sheet of paper from which the phony Connecticut bill had been cut.

The constable arrested a number of Derby residents, including Gideon Washborn, in whose house one of the presses had been set up; the blacksmith Daniel Tucker, who fashioned tools used by the gang; Silvester Wooster, who built the press used to print the bills; Jeremiah Ocain, who traveled to New York to buy copper needed for plates; and William Clark, who had gone to Boston to purchase ink.

Weed, Wooster, and Tucker were sentenced to prison. When he was released some years later, Tucker returned to Derby a chastened man, or as he put it, of "humble and upright behaviour."

On September 8, 1760, the long, wearisome wars against the French ended when Montreal surrendered to a British force commanded by Jeffrey Amherst. In those days communication was slow and it was not until Sunday morning a week or so later that a messenger rode down along the Housatonic River from Albany with the joyous news.

The messenger arrived at the Green at Ripton shortly before the start of morning services, at which a newborn infant was to be baptized. "For a moment he drew rein at the steps of the meetinghouse," wrote Jane De Forest Shelton in *The Salt-Box House,* "while

Tradition holds that David Wooster was born of Abraham and Mary Wooster in 1710 in one of the rear ells of the family homestead in the Pine Rock section of Shelton. Later members of the Wooster family lived in the main house, which was built in the 1740s. Pictured here around the turn of the century, the structure burned down in the early 1900s, and Lenny's Dog House now stands on this historic site. Courtesy, Derby Historical Society

he told the pastor, the Reverend Jedidiah Mills, and the people, the story of the great victory of the English . . . When the courier had vanished . . . the congregation gathered in the meeting-house for worship and thanksgiving, but before these could proceed the child must be baptized. The aged minister, dipping his hand in the water and placing it on the child's forehead, forgot apparently the family name it was to bear, and said, 'Victory, I baptize thee.'"

The joy of that baptismal day, unfortunately, faded even before the child, Victory, grew to an adult, for within a few years relations between England and its American colonies had deteriorated to the point where some men spoke openly of rebellion against the very country under whose flag they had so recently fought.

The Lower Naugatuck Valley did not cherish taking up the sword against England. As late as autumn 1774, when eastern Connecticut towns were aflame with talk of military action against the British, a town meeting in Derby adopted a relatively moderate resolution praising the actions of the Continental Congress then meeting in Philadelphia as "most likely to effect the much to be desired union between Great Britain and the American colonies."

The town meeting approved the plan adopted in Philadelphia for a suspension of trade with Great Britain, voted to establish a committee to make sure that local people did not violate that policy, and agreed to contribute to the relief of the citizens of Boston, whose harbor had been closed by Parliament.

The resolution may have been mild, but the patriotic party unquestionably was in control. When Jonathan Miles, who lived in the Bungay section of what is now Seymour, refused to join a fast ordered by Congress, he was proscribed as an enemy to his country and forced to flee to New York, leaving behind a wife and three young children.

And in December 1775, after hostilities around Boston had ended any chance of reconciliation, the Anglican minister at Derby, the Reverend Richard Mansfield, got himself

into even more serious difficulty when a letter he had written to the British authorities at New York fell into the hands of the patriots.

In the letter the minister had injudiciously "enclosed a list of the names of about ninety persons, heads of families, who were known to be loyalists in Derby and Oxford, and I also gave it as my opinion that several thousand men in the three Western Counties of the Colony would forthwith join the King's army, in case such an army should come over to reduce the Colony to obedience and subjection to his Majesty's Government." Warned that the letter had been intercepted, Mansfield was able to flee to Long Island just a step ahead of the Committee of Inspection.

However indiscreet he was, the Anglican clergyman was undoubtedly on the mark when he suggested that the residents of the

Fleeing deportation from their Nova Scotian homeland in the 1750s, many Acadian refugees fled south to the British colonies. Of the 406 families who ended up in the Connecticut colony, some 30 families were assigned to the Lower Naugatuck Valley. Courtesy, National Archives of Canada

Lower Naugatuck Valley were by no means unanimous in support of the rebellion.

To be sure, the Valley contributed its share of patriotic heroes. At the outbreak of hostilities, a company of 32 Derby men, led by Major Jabez Thompson and Captain Nathaniel Johnson, marched off to join the army assembling near Boston under General Washington.

The old warhorse, General David Wooster, gave up his British army pension to espouse the rebel cause and died commanding militiamen in the defense of Danbury against British invaders.

Lieutenant Bradford Steele and Lieutenant Jabez Pritchard, who fought in the battles around New York City, were captured and incarcerated on one of the infamous prison ships in New York harbor. Pritchard died there, and when Steele was released with other POWs in 1778, he commented, "To behold such a company of living skeletons, one might imagine that the prophecy concerning the dry bones had been fulfilled in us."

Colonel William Hull led troops in all the battles in New York and New Jersey and brought a touch of his beloved Naugatuck Valley to the encampment at Valley Forge in the winter of 1777-1778. "The hut we occu-

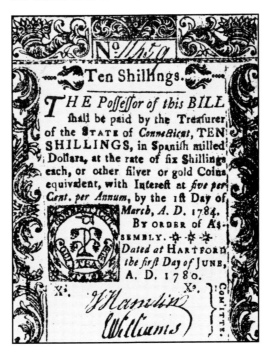

Members of one of the most notorious counterfeiting gangs of early American history were Derby residents Samuel Weed, Gideon Washborn, Daniel Tucker, Silvester Wooster, Jeremiah Ocain, and William Clark. This group generated a conspiracy to print Connecticut and Rhode Island shilling notes such as the one pictured here, but were apprehended when a local Newtown man became suspicious of a Connecticut 20 shilling bill that had been passed to him. Courtesy, Derby Historical Society

News of the French defeat at Montreal and the conclusion of the French and Indian War was delivered to Ripton in 1760 by a messenger on horseback. The news so excited the Reverend Mills that during the ensuing service he absentmindedly baptized a child "Victory." Drawing by Claudia Farkas

pied," he wrote, "consisted of one room. This was dining-room, parlor, kitchen and hall. On one side, shelves were put up for our books, on another stood a row of Derby cheese sent from Connecticut by my mother, a luxury of which the camp could rarely boast."

A number of African-Americans—Jethro Martin, Jethro Freeman, and Quash, among them—took up arms in the cause of independence. Years later, a grateful Derby vouched for the steadfastness of one of them, Tobias Pero. When the selectmen of Woodbury in 1787 ordered Pero to leave their town, apparently thinking he was not a free man, the selectmen of Derby affirmed that he was a citizen who had served his country during the Revolution.

For all of that, some Valley residents were so divided in their loyalties that they fought at one time or another on both sides. Marchant Wooster of Derby served on the patriot side in Colonel Webb's regiment during the campaign of 1776, but,as he put it, "was afterwards unhappily seduced by disaffected persons, a Major French, a British officer, to join the enemy of these States."

Another Derby resident, John Davis, said that he joined the British on Long Island in January 1777 because he had been persuaded "that the British army were so strong and powerful the United States of America would not be able to resist or oppose their march through the country." Davis got more than he bargained for, however, when he was "compelled to take up arms" against the patriots. Unwilling to fight his own countrymen, he "embraced the first opportunity that presented to . . . escape and return to Derby," where he applied for and was granted a pardon.

Although no fighting took place in the Valley, Derby's location as a tidewater port some miles inland made it strategically important as a base for launching operations against British-held Long Island.

Captain Joseph Hull of Huntington, one of the most famous of the whaleboat warriors who made life difficult for the British on Long Island, had his headquarters at Derby. On one occasion Hull, with 20 men concealed in the bottom of his whaleboat, captured a 10-gun, 90-ton British schooner that was taking on a load of provisions near New York. Hull ignored the warnings of the English sentry and got in close enough so that his men could board the schooner. The British crew was subdued and the captain shot. Hull's men hoisted their own whaleboat aboard and set sail under British colors, passing several British armed vessels lying at anchor and bringing their prize safely to Derby.

With its access to farms in the interior of Connecticut, Derby was also important as a supply depot. The patriots maintained warehouses filled with provisions for the Continental Army at the wharves at Derby Landing, and there were suspicions that private citizens with Tory sympathies supplied the British from their own warehouses.

In May 1777, for example, the Americans seized 50 barrels of meat and 100 barrels of flour "collected at Derby and its neighborhood" by Jabez Bacon and Isaac Tomlinson "with a view as was supposed of being transported to the enemy." Bacon and Tomlinson were apprehended and charged with being enemies of the United States.

When the British invaded Danbury in 1777 and New Haven in 1779, it was thought they would attempt to destroy the supplies stored at Derby, so inhabitants of the town turned out to empty the warehouses and secret the provisions. In the 1779 alarm a young lad named Isaac Smith hitched up a wagon and carried load after load to a hollow in what is today the western section of Ansonia. From that day until this, the site has been known as Pork Hollow.

The Valley enjoyed one moment of splendor during the Revolution when the French army, in the spring of 1781, camped on Sentinel Hill overlooking Derby, crossed the Naugatuck and Housatonic rivers, and marched through Ripton en route from Rhode Island to Virginia for the crucial Yorktown campaign that ended any lingering hope the British had of retaining their colonies.

A Derby man, David Humphreys, also had a date with destiny at Yorktown. In 1780 Humphreys was promoted to lieutenant-colonel and appointed aide and secretary to General Washington. At Washington's side throughout the final campaign of the war, Humphreys was selected by the commander in chief to receive the enemy's colors when Lord Cornwallis surrendered, and convey those colors to the Congress in session in Philadelphia.

Upon Humphreys' arrival in Philadelphia, the grateful congressmen voted, "That an elegant sword be presented, in the name of the United States in Congress assembled, to Colonel Humphreys, aide-de-camp to General Washington, to whose care the standards taken under the capitulation of Yorktown were committed, as a testimony of their opinion of his fidelity and ability . . . "

The greater testimony to the fidelity and ability of Humphreys and his comrades was that they had persevered through years of defeats and disappointments and in the end had brought one of the world's major military powers to its knees. Having challenged an empire and won, men like Humphreys looked forward to building a nation.

The Reverend Dr. Richard Mansfield's wife, Anna, while expecting her ninth child, was left to run the Episcopal Glebe House Rectory when her husband was forced to flee to Long Island in 1775. During his absence, which was instigated by his allegiance to the British authorities, both Anna and the infant died at the rectory. The building is pictured here circa 1890. Courtesy, Derby Historical Society

*Shipbuilding at Derby Landing was a prominent indus-
try in the Lower Naugatuck Valley for nearly two centuries, from its inception in the 1600s to its decline in
the 1800s. The launching of handsome ships was a
majestic sight to behold throughout the years. Pictured
here in 1868 is the schooner* Modesty, *a 200-ton vessel
built for Thomas Clapham. It was the last ship to be
constructed at the Hallock shipyards at Derby Landing,
and the people standing on and beside it lend perspective
to its impressive size. Courtesy, Derby Historical Society*

Deeds Not Words

In 1802 Revolutionary War hero David Humphreys returned to the Lower Naugatuck Valley after six years as United States minister to Spain, bringing with him some unlikely traveling companions—91 merino sheep. Farmers from far and near came to see the sheep being unloaded from a sailing ship at Derby Landing, and listen to Humphreys explain how he intended to lay the foundation of a thriving wool industry in the Valley.

Humphreys sold some of the rams and ewes to the farmers, giving them strict instructions on the care and breeding of the animals. Soon the superior qualities of the Spanish sheep became evident. Daniel Holbrook, one of the Derby farmers who purchased a ram, testified that the offspring of that ram, "at shearing yielded one fifth more weight of wool on an average than my other sheep and the quality far superior . . ."

Meanwhile, Humphreys had purchased for $2,647 a tract of land at Chusetown, four-and-a-half miles above Derby where the Naugatuck River passed through a narrow valley and met a natural rock dam that created the 20-foot Rimmon Falls. There, in what is modern-day Seymour, he began laying out the first factory village in the United States—Humphreysville—where the wool from the merino sheep would be converted into cloth. Construction of the woolen mill began early in June 1803, and within a short time an industrial complex was operating: the woolen mill, a four-story cotton factory large enough to contain 2,000 spindles, a clothier's shop, a gristmill, a paper mill, houses that could accommodate 150 workers, and gardens around the factories to provide enough vegetables to feed the entire work force.

Humphreys was determined to avoid the sickness, vice, and illiteracy that plagued European industrial development. He established a school at Humphreysville and paid the schoolmaster's salary. He offered prizes for scholarship and awards for outstanding job performance. He made sure the laborers worked and lived in sanitary conditions, even going before the state legislature and lobbying for a bill requiring that factories be inspected for safety and cleanliness. The colonel also organized a militia company and drilled it himself under the distinctive Humphreysville flag, a blue silk banner showing a merino ewe and ram holding the state seal.

The fame of Humphreys' industrial village was so great that President Jefferson ordered cloth from Humphreysville to make a coat, commenting, "The best fine cloth made in the U.S. is, I am told, at the manufacture of Col. Humphreys . . . " Perhaps more important than presidential praise, however, was the no-nonsense, can-do spirit promoted by Humphreys and his factory town. At one Fourth of July celebration, Humphreys forbade the usual round of windy toasts and instead gave just one toast: "Independence—Deeds not Words. Let those who wish to appear to love their country prove it by actions rather than by toasts and declamations."

While Humphreys was thus striking the spark of industrial development, others were rebuilding the Valley's transportation network and maritime interests, both having fallen into disrepair during the long, weary years of the Revolution. Just before Christmas 1782, a Derby town meeting voted to sponsor a lottery to pay for rebuilding two bridges and constructing a road to Woodbury. The lottery proved not so lucrative as residents had hoped. Only half the tickets were sold, the drawing was postponed, and, in the end, the town had to absorb a portion

of the cost of the work. Still, the work was done and that was what was important.

A few years later Gideon Leavenworth of Huntington, whose family had operated the ferry for years, ran another lottery to finance the first bridge across the Housatonic River from Huntington to Derby. When that lottery fizzled, too, Leavenworth received permission from the state legislature to turn the span into a toll bridge. The toll idea caught on. In 1795 a group of entrepreneurs, following Leavenworth's example, organized the Oxford Turnpike Company, converted the road from Southbury to Chusetown to a toll road, and found the venture so profitable that they got their investment back in two years. All along the route, businesses such as the tavern of Ebenezer Dayton at Chusetown prospered.

When Dayton died, his widow, Phoebe, applied for a license "to retail foreign distilled spirits" and became one of the Valley's first female entrepreneurs. Another enterprising woman in the Valley in those days was Molly Hatchett, one of the last Paugussett Indians to live in Derby. Born in 1738, Hatchett became famous as the originator of a distinctive style of woodsplint basket. She fashioned the baskets and traveled up and down the Valley selling them.

Even with improved roads, the folks in

Huntington and Oxford were beginning to chafe under the necessity of traveling to Stratford and Derby for town meetings. In 1789 Huntington successfully petitioned the General Assembly to become a town. Nine years later the people of Oxford followed suit, asking that they be separated from Derby. When Derby balked at the proposal, the Oxford people packed a town meeting and voted to hold half of all future town meetings at Oxford. Derby residents quickly saw the light, and Oxford became an independent town in October 1798.

The loss of so large a piece of real estate scarcely fazed Derby folks who, literally, had other fish to fry. In 1806 James Lewis, Canfield Gillett, Philo Bassett, and Leman Stone, who had opened a warehouse and store at Derby Landing after the Revolution, secured a charter from the state legislature to form the Derby Fishing Company "for the purpose of prosecuting the Cod and other Fisheries from the Town of Derby . . . " The company raised $50,000, acquired some sailing vessels, received permission to sell maritime insurance, and opened an office in Derby. Shipping notices in New Haven newspapers in the summer of 1810 reveal the diversity and extent of its business: "June 3,

schooner Naugatuck, Capt. Berry, arrived from St. Bartholomew with cargo of rum for the Derby Fishing Company" ; "June 6, brig Victor, Capt. Olmsted, arrived after 16 days from St. Bartholomew with 300 hogshead of rum for the Derby Fishing Co." ; "July 1, schooner Naugatuck, Capt. Berry, sailed for Martinique" ; "July 1, brig Victor, Capt. Elliot, sailed for Antigua" ; "Aug. 11, ship Kesiah, Capt. William Thompson, arrived from St. Ubes after 62 days with salt for the Derby Fishing Company."

The town was such a beehive of commerce that in October 1809 the General Assembly chartered the Valley's first financial institution: the Derby Bank. It was said that on one occasion a fishing company ship brought from New York a chest of specie that required eight men to carry from the dock to the old brick bank building at Derby Narrows. The Reverend Charles Nichols, who grew up in Derby about this time left a vivid description of the prosperity that the shipping business brought to the landing:

There were five or six stores there; also one drug-gist, several coopers, one tanner, one hatter and three or four tailors and shoemakers and joiners and carpenters . . . Ship-building was carried on

there from year to year . . . Indeed it was a grand and beautiful sight to behold when a large vessel that had been months in building . . . was set in motion down an inclined plane, first moving slowly . . . and then more and more rapidly til the sparks of fire from friction would be seen all along her pathway and amid noise and smoke and scores and hundreds of voices cheering, she would strike the water with a splash, plowing up great waves and gliding off as a proud thing of life far into the stream, sitting there for a few moments as if for a thousand eyes to look upon her graceful form and admire her beauty.

Understandably, the merchants and shipbuilders of Derby and Huntington were horrified and outraged when people down-river began talking about throwing a bridge across the river between Stratford and Mil-ford, a bridge that would virtually cut the Valley off from the open sea. Valley people fought the proposal vigorously, but were un-able to prevent the state legislature from granting a charter for the Washington Bridge in 1802. When the bridge was swept away by ice in 1807, Colonel Tomlinson of Hunting-ton broke out his best wine and threw a party, offering a toast, "May the fishing and ship-ping interests of our river never be disturbed by the intolerable nuisance of another bridge across the mouth of its waters."

The colonel was to be disappointed, for Stratford people quickly rebuilt the bridge. One of the first ships to approach it after its reconstruction was a vessel owned by Captain Claudius Bartholomew of Derby. When the bridge attendant insisted upon inspecting Bartholomew's papers before he would open the draw, the short-fused Frenchman loaded his two small cannons with iron spikes and blasted away, splintering the bridge's superstructure. The attendant promptly opened the draw and Bartholo-mew sailed on up to Derby.

In the end, the bothersome bridge did less harm to Valley shipping interests than both the embargo ordered by Presi-dent Jefferson in 1807 and the War of 1812,

In 1789 the parish of Ripton was granted inde-pendence and renamed Huntington in honor of Samuel Huntington. Signer of the Declaration of Independence, president of the Continental Congress (1779-1781), and gover-nor of Connecticut (1786-1796), Huntington was a prominent and leading Connecticut citizen. And perhaps as in the earlier case of Seymour's indepen-dence in 1850, the towns-people of Huntington thought their chance for separation would be en-hanced by assuming the name of the state's current governor. Courtesy, Derby Historical Society

ABOVE: The Incident on the Housatonic *by George T. Ericson of Milford, Connecticut, depicts the confrontation between Captain Claudius Bartholomew of Derby and the bridge sentinel at Stratford, which occurred upon the captain's return from the West Indies. When the sentinel demanded to inspect Bartholomew's papers before raising the draw, the Frenchman loaded his cannon and proceeded to destroy the bridge's superstructure. This minor conflict symbolizes the rivalry that existed between the two port communities during the colonial period. Courtesy, Fagan's Restaurant, Stratford*

not to mention the construction of the New Haven turnpike in 1798 and the Bridgeport turnpike in 1801. But even those dark clouds had their silver linings. The war gave the Valley a great naval hero, Commodore Isaac Hull, who commanded "Old Ironsides," the USS *Constitution,* when it captured the British frigate *Guerriere* off the Gulf of St. Lawrence in August 1812. And the embargo, the war, and the resulting tariff of 1816 forced Americans to build their own industrial base, something for which the Valley,

with its water power, soon proved itself remarkably well suited.

As the early stirrings of industry were felt, the Valley was also experiencing its first partisan politics with the rise of the Jeffersonian Republicans to oppose the entrenched Federalists. The Republicans harped away at such issues as the status of Congregationalism as the state's established religion, the lack of a state constitution, and the stand-up law, which required voters to actually stand up in town meetings and vote for the candidates of their choice.

The Republican, or Toleration, message fell on receptive ears in the Valley. When in the spring of 1817 the Republicans elected Oliver Wolcott as their first governor, Derby, Oxford, and Huntington all voted the Toleration ticket.

Meanwhile, industrialization was proceeding apace. In the 1820s David Clark operated a tailoring business in Oxford, employing a number of workers to produce clothing to be sold in the South. And in what today is Beacon Falls, Thomas Sanford, in 1834, invented and manufactured friction matches.

That same year a Derby native, Sheldon Smith, started a manufacturing village,

LEFT: On September 1, 1833, Shelton Smith saw the first shovelful of earth moved to begin construction of the Birmingham canal system. The canal was to provide the necessary power for the development of the new manufacturing village in Derby. The project was so successful that it was the impetus for the Lower Naugatuck Valley's transformation to an industrial economy. This circa 1875 picture shows the Birmingham Iron Foundry buildings on the far side of the canal, with the Howe Pin factory at the far end. The buildings closest to the river comprise the Alling Mills facility on the site of the original Phelps Copper location. Courtesy, Derby Public Library

FACING PAGE, BOTTOM LEFT: Commodore Isaac Hull was 40 when he married the lovely 23-year-old Anna M. Hart of Old Saybrook on January 2, 1813. The wedding was held in New York City just four and a half months after Hull's famous victory over the Guerriere. Courtesy, Derby Historical Society

FACING PAGE, BOTTOM RIGHT: Born at Derby Landing on March 9, 1773, Commodore Isaac Hull, who commanded the USS Constitution during the War of 1812, was the third son of Joseph Hull IV. This 1807 painting by Gilbert Stuart preceded the great naval battle between the USS Constitution and the frigate Guerriere by five years. Courtesy, Derby Historical Society

Smithville, or Birmingham as it came to be known, on the west side of the Naugatuck, north of Derby Landing. His success in harnessing the Naugatuck River's water power soon attracted other industrialists.

In the spring of 1836 Edward N. Shelton and his brother-in-law Nathan C. Sanford built the first tack factory in the nation. About the same time, D.W. Plumb and Benjamin Beach built their woolen factory, and David Bassett his auger factory. Anson G. Phelps, a New York capitalist, established a factory for manufacturing sheet copper and copper wire.

One visitor, Elliott Sargent, wrote his brother in Northampton, Massachusetts, about the state-of-the-art technology being used in the new industrial village: "Mother, Andrew, Henry and myself went to Birmingham and visited [the] pin [factory] and tack factory and also saw the sheet brass made . . . [At the pin factory] the brass wire goes into the machine and is cut to proper length. It is then carried round by the same machine and so sharpened. And then a part of the machine which looks like a pair of fingers hands it to another part and the head is made. It is then dropped down into a bucket. To whiten them, they are silvered over, I believe, though we did not see the process. It is quite curious to see them put upon the papers. This is done by girls with a machine."

The rapid growth of Birmingham en-

RATES OF FREIGHT

FOR 1847, BETWEEN

DERBY, MILFORD, STRATFORD,

AND

NEW YORK,

BY THE STEAMERS OF THE

Naugatuck Transportation Company.

Boxes & Bales of Merchandise, pr ft.	0.04	Hides, dry,		3 to 0.04
" Clocks and light boxes, "	0.02 1-2	" salted,		6 to 0.08
" " Weights, each	0.07	Horses, each,		1.50
" Soap,	0.10	Pig Iron, Copper and Spelter, } per 2000 lbs.		1.50
" Tin Plate,	0.12 1-2			
" Candles,	0.10	Bar Iron, Steel and Old Copper, } per 2000 lbs.		1.50
" Pipes,	0.08			
" Raisins,	4 to 0.06	Kegs of Tobacco,		10 to 0.20
" Spice, &c.	6 to 0.10	Lime, per barrel,		0.17
" Lemons and Oranges, each	0.12 1-2	Cement, "		0.20
" Glass,	6 to 0.08	Leather, per side,		0.03
" Havana Sugar,	0.37 1-2	" per roll,		10 to 0.20
" Lump "	0.25	Metals, manufactured, in boxes or casks, } per 2000 lbs.		2.00
" Metal and Cloth Buttons, each	0.10			
Bales of Cotton, each	37 1-2 to 0.50	Nails, per keg,		0.12 1-2
" Sheeting, "	15 to 0.25	" per ton,		1.50
Bundles of Sheet Iron, per 100 lbs.	0.10	Oil in barrels		0.25
" Russia " " "	0.10	" tierces,		0.50
Brooms, per doz.	0.10	" hhds.		75 cts. to 1.00
Boards, White Pine, per M.	1.50	Packages of Axes,		0.12 1-2
" Mahogany, Cherry, &c.	3.00	Paper, per 2000 lbs.		2.00
Bags Coffee, Cocoa, &c.	0.12 1-2	Pitchforks, per doz.		0.08
" Shot,	0.04	Planks and Timber, per M.		2 to 3.00
Barrels of Sugar,	0.18 3-4	Plough Timbers, &c. pr carman load,		1.00
" Flour,	0.18 3-4	Rags, pressed, per 2000 lbs.		1.50
" do. if over 5 bbls.	0.12 1-2	" not pressed,		2.00
" Crackers and Wood Ware,	0.18	Salt, in large sacks,		0.20
" Dye Stuffs,	15 to 0.25	" small "		0.03
" Liquor,	0.25	" " " if over 50 sacks,		0.02 1-2
" Pork and Beef,	0.25	Scythes, per doz.		0.06 1-4
Bricks, per M.	2 to 3.00	Shovels and Spades, per doz.		0.10
do. Fire,	4.00	Springs and Axles, per 2000 lbs.		2.00
Cheese, per 2000 lbs.	2.00	Saddle Trees, per doz.		0.06 1-4
Cattle, each,	1.50 to 2.00	Staves, Hhd. per M.		3.00
Crates of Crockery, per foot,	0.02	" Pipe,		4.00
Carriages,	75 cts. to 3.00	" Barrel,		2.00
Carboys,	0.30	Shooks, per bundle,		0.08
Chairs, Fancy, per bundle,	0.08	Stoves,		15 to 0.34
" Seats, per doz.	0.05	Nest Casks,		0.30
Chests of Tea,	6 to 0.15	Tierces of Rice,		0.37 1-2
Firkins of Butter and Lard,	8 to 0.12	" Potash, per 100 lbs.		0.07 1-2
Fish, per cwt.	0.12 1-2	Tin Ware, in boxes and casks, pr foot,		0.02
Flax Seed, per tierce,	0.30	White Lead, in kegs, per 2000 lbs.		2.00
Grapes, per keg,	0.10	Wire, in bundles, per 100 lbs.		0.10
Ginger, per keg,	0.10	Wool, per 100 lbs.		0.12 1-2
Grain, per bushel,	4 to 0.05	All heavy goods, not enumerated above, } per 2000 lbs.		2.00
Hhds. of Sugar,	75 cts. to 1.00			
Hhds. of Melasses,	75 cts. to 1.00	Small and single packages,		0.12 1-2

N. B. No goods delivered until the Freight is paid, except in cases of special contract.

Hotchkiss & Newson, Printers, Birmingham.

"one of the finest places for a village in this western world." The new town was named Ansonia, a Latinized version of Phelps' first name.

Flushed with the success of Birmingham, some Valley businessmen, led by Edward N. Shelton of Huntington, organized the Naugatuck Transportation Company in 1843 and commissioned the building of a 120-ton, iron-hulled steamboat—christened the *Naugatuck*, but known to Valley people as the "Iron Pot" —and revived the New York to Derby service that had been tried in 1824, but dropped for want of business.

An economic survey completed by the state in 1845 gave ample evidence of the fruits of all this activity. On the west side of the Housatonic River, Huntington remained the most rural of the Valley towns. Its agricultural products, ranging from Indian corn to tobacco to cider to goose feathers, were valued at $62,282, while its manufactures were valued at a mere $31,051. Most of its factories employed only one or two people, suggesting that they were probably for the most part home industries. One of the major revenue producers in Huntington was fishing. Huntington anglers caught 32,200 shad valued at $4,693 from the Housatonic and an undisclosed number of other fish valued at $1,000.

Oxford was somewhat more industrialized than Huntington. Sixty-nine Oxford residents were employed in three woolen mills, a screw factory, a hat factory, a chair factory, and various small industries that manufactured products valued at $72,111. Overall, however, Oxford retained much of its rural flavor, its farms producing 11,000 bushels of Indian corn, 14,685 bushels of potatoes, 36,020 pounds of butter, and 19,235 pounds of cheese.

Derby—with its factory villages of Humphreysville, Birmingham, and Ansonia—had virtually lost any semblance of an agricultural community. Its farms produced a mere $29,514 worth of agricultural goods, while its factories employed 900 residents—more

couraged Phelps to expand the village to the north. He was blocked, however, by a crotchety property owner named Stephen Booth who kept upping the price of his land. Exasperated, Phelps chose instead to cross to the east side of the Naugatuck River, where he selected a site that his surveyor proclaimed, with perhaps a bit of hyperbole,

than 200 of them women—and turned out goods valued at almost $1 million annually. At the Anson Phelps factory, 40 employees produced 1.2 millon pounds of copper products valued at $275,000. In his foundry and machine shop, Almon Farrel supervised 30 workers who cast 300 tons of brass and iron products valued at $30,000. Eighty workers at the town's three woolen mills turned out 500,000 yards of cloth, 91,520 yards of cotton yarn, and 4,000 yards of cotton batting. Two paper factories employed 12 men and 6 women and produced 225 tons of paper, much of it newsprint for New Haven newspapers. One hundred dozen axes valued at $47,500 were produced by 47 workers at two factories. Twenty-eight employees produced 350,000 pounds of tacks and brads valued at $35,000, and 40 workers produced 150,000 pounds of pins valued at $60,000.

The figures were enough to encourage a young journalist, Thomas M. Newson, to launch the Valley's first newspaper, the *Derby Journal*, on Christmas Day 1846, with the optimistic comment, "When we consider that there are now manufacturing villages constantly springing into existence and the

growth and importance of the places about us are daily increasing, we cannot but believe there is at least some grounds for encouragement if not an almost certainty of eventually succeeding . . . "

Others were being drawn to the Valley by the same potential that Newson saw. John Limburner, a native of Kilmarnock, Scotland, came to Derby and practiced his trade as a cooper in the flourishing shipping business. From his native Leeds in England, Thomas Gilyard came to Humphreysville to work in the clothing factory. A master at mixing dyes, Gilyard was said to be the first broadcloth finisher in America.

A Welshman, Thomas Ellis, found not only a job but also religion in the Valley. He came to Humphreysville as a spinner in the cotton mills and earned a reputation as a wild young fellow with a golden voice who would often sing the night away in local taverns. Then he was converted to Methodism and he turned his voice to serving the Lord rather than singing bawdy melodies.

Another Valley newcomer who put his voice to good use was John W. Osborne, a native of New Haven. As a lad, Osborne

FACING PAGE: Organization of the Naugatuck Transportation Company by Valley businessmen in 1843 revived freight service between Derby and New York. This 1847 rate sheet provides an excellent overview of items that were shipped in the area, including wire, wool, tea, and tobacco. Courtesy, Derby Public Library

The old paddleboat Stamford *was one of a number of steamboats that plied the waters of the Housatonic River from Derby to New York, carrying passengers and freight from 1824 until 1889. The* Sentinel *described this period of development as a "colorful, spasmodic, 65-year era of whistle, sputter and splash." Courtesy, Derby Historical Society*

The Ansonia Clock Company joined the ranks of new Naugatuck Valley industries in 1850, and proceeded to spread the name of Ansonia across the country and around the world. The company later moved to Brooklyn in 1879, and a display of its products is shown here at the Chicago Exposition of 1893. Courtesy, Ansonia Public Libary

RIGHT: Viewing the growth of the Birmingham and Ansonia sections of Derby, a correspondent of the New Haven Palladium *saw in their development a new metropolis on the horizon. "New Haven," he stated, "will no longer be without a fair competitor." Courtesy, Derby Historical Society*

earned his first spending money by singing patriotic songs of the Revolution and the War of 1812 for the Valley militiamen on training days. Osborne, too, was eventually converted to Methodism, which was making great inroads at that time, and became director of the church choir.

Slavery was a dying institution in the Valley in the early years of the 19th century, but African-Americans often remained as servants to white folks. One black woman, Nancy Freeman, years later recounted her life story: "When I was nine years old, I went to live with Mr. Truman Coe, up in Coe's Lane, on Derby Hill, and if I staid till I was nineteen I was to have a cow and a feather bed . . . The way it was, when I was sixteen Roswell [Freeman] come and asked if I would accept of his company and I accepted of it. But I stayed till I was 18 and I got my cow and then I staid another year and I got my feather bed . . . " Nancy and Roswell Freeman eventually were married in the parlor of the Coe home, she in "a white muslin dress all worked over with little dots, low neck and short sleeves, and white silk gloves, and white stockings and low blue prunell shoes and a white silk

handkerchief around my neck."

Roswell Freeman enjoyed a reputation as one of the best fox hunters in the Valley. He was called "the farmer's benefactor" and the board on which he dressed skins showed marks for 331 foxes.

It was customary for black folks throughout New England to celebrate as one of their annual holidays a mock election day in which they picked a governor, and Freeman was one of the governors of the Valley. Another governor was Juba Weston of Humphreysville, a slave of Colonel Humphreys. Weston's sons, Nelson and Wilson, also served as governors, the latter apparently being the last to serve, in the years just before the Civil War.

On such occasions as the election of a Negro governor and the observance of George Washington's birthday, it was the custom of Valley folks to dance the night away. On February 25, 1847, the *Journal* reported that, despite a heavy snowstorm several days before, a ball at Moshier's Hotel in Humphreysville "went off in fine style and everyone seemed to enjoy the occasion . . . The dance continued until morning . . . the 22nd was also celebrated by a number of our citizens who assembled together and partook of the luxuries of a well-spread table pre-

The Home Woolen Mill has been the central industrial complex in Beacon Falls since it was first built in the 1800s. Later the Rubber Shoe Company and today a condominium association, the facility remains a key historical landmark. Courtesy, Charles Rotteck

pared in Moshier's choicest style . . . everything passed off in such a manner as to render the 22nd of February 1847 a day not soon to be forgotten."

Some people thought that levity and license were getting out of hand in the Valley. At their annual meeting later that same year, members of the Derby Temperance Society heard an alarming report. More than $270 had been spent by the town to prosecute

cases originating from rum during the year, the report indicated, and such cases were rapidly increasing, 24 cases being prosecuted before one justice of the peace in Birmingham between June 15 and August 21. In addition, "Not only are our young men led into the habit of drinking, but . . . gambling with all its train of attendant vices prevails to an extent little dreamed of by many . . . "

Whatever its problems, the Valley in the first half of the nineteenth century had become a region to be reckoned with. So impressed was a correspondent of the *New Haven Palladium* after a visit to Derby, Birmingham, and Ansonia in the late 1840s that he predicted the three would one day become a single city rivaling New Haven as Connecticut's preeminent metropolis. "Thus peeping forth on each other with maiden bashfulness from their wildwood homes on the hillside and through the valley," he wrote, waxing eloquent, "these three fond sister villages in harmony dwell . . . and I trust one day they will meet and thenceforth know a single name, a single interest and a single destiny. When this union shall take place, New Haven will no longer be without a fair competitor."

Colonel William B. Wooster, son of Russell and Avis Burr Wooster of Oxford, led the campaign against the petition to grant separate town status to Ansonia on behalf of the West Ansonians. Wooster was defeated, however, when the bill was signed into law on April 15, 1889. Wooster is shown here with his wife, daughter of pioneer brass manufacturer Thomas Wallace, as they ready for an afternoon ride. Courtesy, Derby Historical Society

A New Epic

At precisely half past four o'clock on Thursday afternoon last," reported the *Derby Journal* on May 17, 1849, ". . . the visage of the iron horse was visible just beyond Derby Landing and before our citizens could say Jack Robinson . . . he bounded like an enraged maniac followed by his train of gloomy looking cars. After roaming around as far as the ville [Humphreysville], he took it into his head to return and back he came . . . The appearance of the monster was certainly a new epic in the history of Derby."

A new epic, indeed. An epic in which the rural life of the valley would retreat steadily before the pressure of Industrial Revolution technology.

The old ways might still prevail occasionally, as was the case shortly after the Naugatuck Railroad opened, when the *Journal* reported, "On Friday, the freight train 'down' was turning a curve about a mile and a half this side of Naugatuck. The locomotive suddenly came upon a large cow, which threw the engine off the track, down an embankment about 30 feet into the river, killing the fireman and severely bruising the engineer. The locomotive and the baggage car were so much injured that they probably will be of no further use."

But in the long run, the new technology was going to turn the Valley into an industrial colossus. As early as 1846, when the railroad was still in the talking stages, some Derby men saw what was coming and organized the Derby Savings Bank to provide the capital necessary for industrial growth. Within five years a host of other banks sprang up to meet the demand for investment capital: the Young Men's Savings Bank and Building Association in Seymour, which had shed its old name of Humphreysville; the People's Savings Bank and the Manufac-

turer's Bank in Birmingham; and the Ansonia Savings Bank.

The need for capital was matched by a need for labor, and the construction of the railroad brought with it a large-scale influx of foreign workers—Irishmen fleeing famine in their native land and happy for any opportunity to earn a living.

Some found only a grave in their adopted home. During construction of the railroad, a landslide several miles above Derby buried two of them. One survived, but the other, a native of County Cork, "was found dead having been underground nearly 45 minutes," reported the *Journal*. Others were victimized by unscrupulous contractors. In Seymour, John R. Woodbury, a subcontractor on the rail line, absconded with a $4,000 payroll. "Our streets," reported the *Journal*'s Seymour correspondent, "are swarmed with Irish who have lost nearly a quarter's wages. Some of them have declared that nothing but his life will satisfy them if they ever catch him . . . " Despite the hardships, many of the Irishmen found the valley a good place to put down roots.

So, too, did some skilled German craftsmen who settled in Beacon Falls, which was a thriving little community long before it was incorporated in 1871. In January 1858 *The National Magazine* wrote, "The small cluster of houses and the large manufacturing establishment known . . . as Beacon Falls Station are most picturesquely situated in the midst of some of the wildest scenery of this portion of Connecticut . . . A great variety of articles are manufactured here . . . "

The newcomers weren't always welcome, especially the Irish. When the Know-Nothing party came to power in the state in 1855, Governor William T. Minor went so far as to order the disbanding of all Irish militia units, one of them from Derby, on the grounds that their loyalty was suspect.

Distrust of the Irish, however, was soon forgotten amid more substantial questions of loyalty. When the nation teetered on the brink of a sectional split during the 1860 presidential campaign, Charles Russell, a tack factory foreman, was a leader of the Derby Wide Awakes, a group of radical Republicans supporting Abraham Lincoln. At one rally, Russell was asked what the country would be like in 1864. "Before that day," he replied prophetically, "this country will run red with blood." Russell didn't live to see 1864. He died on February 8, 1862, leading his 10th Connecticut Regiment in an assault on Confederate defenses at Roanoke Island, North Carolina.

Like Russell, hundreds of Valley men went off to fight and die in such places as Fredericksburg, Harper's Ferry, Atlanta, and Andersonville.

Derby's David B. Rowell, a private in Company B of the 20th Regiment, perhaps expressed the sentiments of most of the volunteers when he wrote in a letter in December 1862, "I like soldiering very well considering what a damn fool I was to enlist." Two years later, Rowell was killed when a band of Confederate guerrillas attacked the 20th Regiment's camp at Tracy City, Tennessee.

Rock formations like this one pictured south of Ansonia, circa 1850, were challenging hurdles to those laying the tracks for each of the railroads constructed in the Naugatuck Valley. Irish immigrants provided the main work force in the building of the Naugatuck Line, and many persons living today can still recall the echo of the steam whistle, which announced the approaching trains. Courtesy, Derby Historical Society

Not all Valley folks were as zealous for the Union cause as Russell and Rowell. It was said that at one time opponents of the war—Copperheads as they were called—raised a Confederate flag over the Oxford green. The Copperheads also frequently harassed the Reverend George Lansing Taylor, the abolitionist pastor of the Seymour Methodist Church, serenading the clergyman and his wife in the middle of the night with the ditty, "We'll hang Parson Taylor to a sour apple tree, as we go marching on."

In March 1863 Taylor's wife was instrumental in the founding of the Soldier's Aid Society, which gathered clothing and medical supplies and shipped them off to the troops. Her timing was good, for that spring the Army of the Potomac had need of all the supplies it could get its hands on when it took a bad licking at Chancellorsville and then fought the rebels to a bloody standoff in the decisive Gettysburg campaign.

A Valley soldier, Corporal Wales Terrell of Derby, described in his diary the carnage

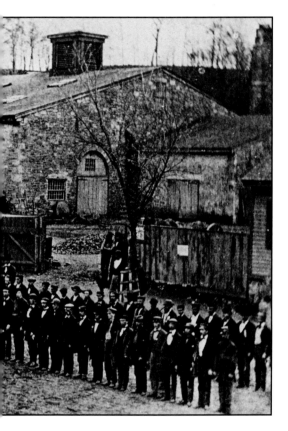

of Gettysburg and what is often referred to as the high water mark for the Confederacy—Pickett's futile charge against the Union lines on Cemetery Ridge on July 3.

"They came on," wrote Terrell, "like an army of iron men, as brave as brave could be . . . Our artillery reserved their fire until they came within a few hundred feet and then they opened with a deadly withering blast. And how wicked it was. Brave men fell like grass before the mower's scythe . . . "

On the rainy Sunday after the Confederates had retreated into Maryland, Terrell wandered over the desolate battlefield and wrote, "Traded shoes and stockings with one of our enemy; his were good and mine were played out. It was an even swap and a case where it took but one to make a bargain."

When the war ended, soldiers returning to the Valley popularized baseball, a sport that had been played in the camps of both armies. The Valley had a number of teams as early as 1866—the Unions of Beacon Falls, the Birmingham Baseball and

Quoit Club (which seems to have played under the jazzier name of Qui Vives), a nameless Ansonia nine that got whipped 50-30 by the New Haven West End Club, and the Seymour Americans, whose 61-40 victory over Naugatuck on June 1, 1866, was duly noted in the *Waterbury American*, accompanied by what may have been the first box score of a Valley baseball game.

The same year a Frenchman named Pierre Lallement and an Irish-American named James Carroll secured a patent for a recreational vehicle known as a "velocipede," and Lallement is said to have put this early bicycle through its paces on the streets of Ansonia and Derby.

In winter the more bucolic pastimes continued to hold sway. "Almost every hillside is made subservient to sport . . . by boys and girls who ply their sleds up and down making old winter merry and frolicsome," reported the *Journal* in mid-January 1868. Sometimes the youngsters became too frolicsome, for in 1881 Seymour adopted an ordinance banning sledding on certain roads. The town meeting at which the ordinance

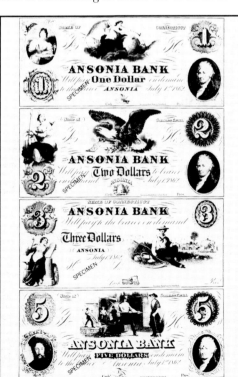

LEFT: Local citizens responded to Abraham Lincoln's call for volunteers, and November 1861 saw Company B of the First Regiment of Connecticut Volunteers gathered in front of the old Copper Mill at Main and Tremont streets in Ansonia under the command of Captain Elisha S. Kellogg. After achieving the rank of colonel, Kellogg was later killed at Cold Harbor, Virginia, on June 1, 1864, while serving with the Second Regiment of the Connecticut Volunteers. Courtesy, Ansonia Public Library

The need for investment capital grew with the introduction of the railroad and its ensuing industrial development. Numerous banks were established to meet the growing demand for financial services, and larger banking institutions opened local branches in the Naugatuck Valley as well. These replicas of 1862 currency from the Ansonia Bank, a branch of the Union and New Haven Trust Company, feature the image of local hero David Humphreys. Courtesy, Derby Historical Society

Lieutenant Hiram Upson of Seymour of Company F, Seventh Regiment, Connecticut Volunteers, gave his life in the Civil War. He enlisted on August 29, 1861, and was mortally wounded at the battle of James Island, South Carolina, on June 16, 1862, and died just two days later. Upson Post, No. 40 of the G.A.R. was established in his honor. Courtesy, Derby Historical Society

classes in musical gymnastics for young and old in both Birmingham and Ansonia. The *Journal* was enthusiastic: "We heartily recommend the classes for both sexes and think [their] general introduction into our schools would be beneficial."

There was similar enthusiasm a few years later when Dana Bartholomew and George C. Allis announced they were going to bring some culture to the Valley by sponsoring what the *Derby Transcript* described as "a series of first-class entertainments at the Ansonia Opera House." Special trains were to be run on the Derby Railroad for the performances and "the best seats in the opera house will be apportioned equitably" between Ansonia and Derby. The first performance, billed as "undoubtedly the greatest concert ever given in this vicinity," was to feature the famous pianist, Madam Julia Reed King.

Madam King didn't live up to her billing, or as the *Transcript* rather abruptly put it, "She was not in tune." But then, the Valley didn't seem to be ready for too much culture anyway, for Madam King's incompetence was "partially excused," suggested the *Transcript*, "through the utter want of breeding of a portion of her audience who cared nothing for the pleasure of others, but disturbed the concert by talking or getting up to go out at the most inopportune times."

Valley folks were much more at home with old-fashioned amusements. A strawberry festival sponsored by the Congregational Church in Oxford in July 1866 attracted such a large crowd, said the *New Haven Register*, "that very many were unable to get a glimpse of the fair damsels whose countenances beamed at the rapidity with which the rare fruit and cream, rich cake

was proposed was a raucous one. "There were about fifty present," said the *New Haven Register*, "and the coasters and anti-coasters were about equally divided. There was considerable filibustering . . . one attempt being made to postpone the matter until July 4."

Another winter pastime was aerobics, albeit under a different name. In 1867 a young lady named Miss King organized

One favorite recreational activity for area residents was a boating excursion on Sunday afternoons. Here, a group of friends are about to depart in their canopied leisure boat for a ride on the Housatonic River to view Shelton, Seymour, Derby, and Oxford from the water in the late 1800s. Courtesy, Dorothy Tanner

and pie, heaping glasses of lemonade, etc. disappeared."

Independence Day was celebrated in Beacon Falls, according to the *Transcript*'s description, with a sort of townwide family picnic: "The 4th was duly ushered into existence by a national salute from the Beacon Falls Light Battery. At sunrise the Ragmuffins of Capt. Bradley, paraded the streets of our village . . . At 10 a.m., a procession of the same group and Sunday scholars and citizens formed, led by Mr. Wolfe of the Home Woolen Company and Dr. Munson . . . with drums beating, fifes screaming and colors flying through the principal streets to the grounds just west of the village where the day was spent in social enjoyments."

Beacon Falls was also the site of the Valley's first amusement park, High Rock Grove, which was constructed by the Naugatuck Railroad as an inducement for excursions. The entrance to the grove was embellished by a floral arrangement of the letters HRG, and the grounds included such attractions as an archery range, a roller-skating rink, swings, croquet grounds, and a

restaurant. The crowning attraction, literally, was a pavilion 125 feet above the grove itself, built, the *Waterbury American* declared, "on the extreme point of the cliff on the very point where the forest red man set his lookout watch hundreds of years ago."

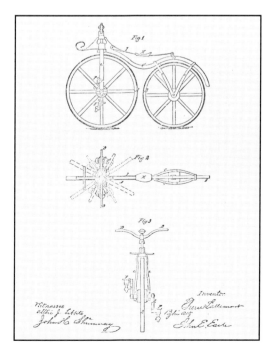

Pierre Lallement was issued the first bicycle patent in the country on November 22, 1866, for his invention called the velocipede. Prior to his application, Lallement had tested this new mode of transportation along Main Street in Ansonia, over the long covered bridge, and down the country road south to the village of Birmingham and back again. Courtesy, Derby Historical Society

One of the Valley's perennial entertainers in these years was the Yankee Fiddler, Sheldon Lake. Each autumn Lake meandered down along the Housatonic River, doing odd jobs for farmers by day and fiddling at barn dances and corn huskings in Oxford, Derby, and Shelton in the evening.

Shelton remained largely a rural community until the early 1870s, when the Ousatonic Water Company, the brainchild of Edwin N. Shelton, overcame the objections of shad fishermen and built a dam across the Housatonic River.

The dam was opened on October 10, 1870, with a great parade and much fanfare. The marshal of the day, Doctor Ambrose Beardsley, paid tribute to a project "which now guarantees to this locality a water power scarcely equaled in the whole country . . . Factories, mansions and temples of worship, neat little cottages, beautiful parks, verdant lawns and spacious avenues, teeming with a population of life and activity, will rise up here . . . "

The doctor was a good prophet. "Since the completion of the Ousatonic Dam in 1870," commented *The Historical, Statistical and Industrial Review of the State of Connecticut*, published in 1883, "Shelton has grown rapidly, and there are now in operation 15 factories, among which is the Derby Silver Company employing four hundred hands and the cotton mills, which run 12,000 spindles and 300 looms. There are many other manufactures here, which include corsets, carriages, hardware, pins, paper boxes, etc. There is also a large paper mill; also a brass mill and foundry . . . "

The same directory reveals an amazing diversity of manufacturing throughout the Valley. On Canal Street in Shelton, E.C. Maltby employed 60 workers producing an odd combination of Britannia flatware and desiccated coconut. In Seymour, the New Haven Copper Company was the largest producer of bath-tub copper in the nation, and Colonel Humphreys' old firm, the Humphreysville Mfg. Co., had turned to the manufacture of cast-steel augurs and bits. In Derby the five-story Birmingham Corset Co. employed 300 workers, while James N. Wise's confectionery had earned a statewide reputation by manufacturing "ice cream frozen by water power." In Ansonia the S.O. & C. Co. was so technologically advanced that one employee using a machine "can eyelet 300 to 400 dozen corsets in ten hours, with minimum outlay of labor on his part, setting all

the eyelets perfectly and without any waste."

The Valley was also becoming a veritable United Nations. In a factory on Main Street in Ansonia, 17 employees produced cigars under the watchful eye of A. Martinez, a native of Malaga, Spain. On the same street, two Scots, John H. Shaw and John R. Murray, ran a dry goods store; E.J. Buckley, "a native of the Emerald Isle," conducted a sign-painting business; and the three Hassard sisters, "from the North of Ireland," ran a dressmaking shop. On High Street, a Frenchman named Thomas Cryshie, a linguist fluent in English, German, Russian, Polish, Turkish, Wallachian, and Greek, ran a tailor's shop. A German named B. Goodman employed 40 workers at his buckle factory, and his fellow countryman, John B. Gardner, employed an equal number manufacturing clock dials and trimmings.

The Valley's black community was also growing. In Ansonia, Wallace and Sons—where William Wallace had invented the first electric arc light in the country—had so

many orders to supply brass cartridges for the Russian army that it sent one of its black employees, Jim Marshall, to Washington, D.C., to recruit other black workers. In June 1881, 32 of these workmen created quite a stir in Ansonia, said the *New Haven Register*, when they "got off the morning train and marched double file through Main Street. The citizens wondered what brought such a number into town so early and all

The Birmingham Iron Foundry, located in Birmingham in 1836, first grew under the leadership of the Colburns and later the Bassetts and the Wannings, and by 1889 played a major role in the production of machinery for the India rubber industry. Courtesy, Ansonia Public Library

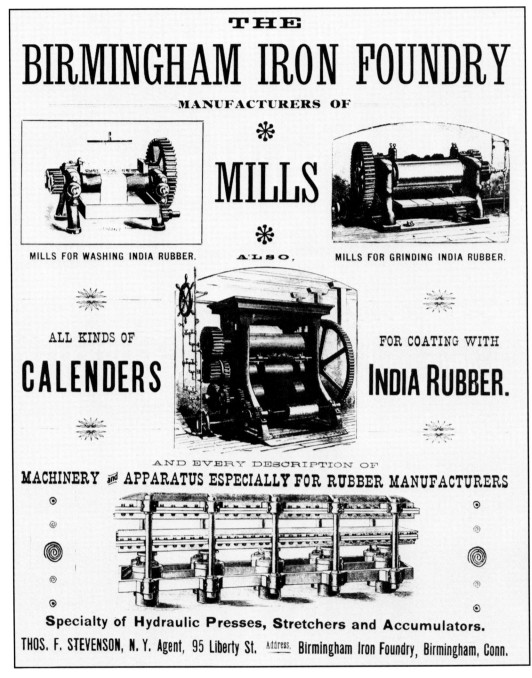

watched their destination with interest." One of the black men told a reporter that they wouldn't work for less than what all the other employees were getting at the Wallace plant and that more blacks would come in a short time if they were satisfied with the working conditions.

Wages and working conditions were the concern of all the employees of the Val-

ley's growing industries, and in time that concern led to organized labor and confrontations with management. One of the earliest and most bitter of these was the strike at the Derby Silver Co. in early 1886.

With the issues ranging from a demand for a pay increase to an end to the practice of charging the workmen 5 percent interest on money drawn by them, the strike pitted the Knights of Labor against the company. When the company brought in strike breakers, violence erupted. "A crowd of scabs," reported the *New Haven Union* on March 5, "entered a Main Street saloon [in Birmingham] where they drank freely. In the saloon at the time were a number of strikers. Taunting remarks on both sides led to threats and then to blows. In a very short time, a general free fight was in progress, chairs and tables were smashed, bottles and glasses were thrown and quite a number of the participants are reported to have been badly bruised." The strike finally was settled at the beginning of April with the company estimating that it had lost $25,000.

Confrontations weren't limited to labor relations. The publication of the first comprehensive history of the Valley, *The History of the Old Town of Derby, Connecticut, 1642-1880*, by Samuel Orcutt and Ambrose Beardsley,

author of the Derby History."

The next week Beardsley, who obviously was the one responsible for "Ousatonic" rather than "Housatonic," responded. He complained about the editing and publishing of the book and commented sarcastically about Orcutt: "If his mortification is more decided than mine for having joined in partnership with him in the publication of the history, I pity him."

As sharp as it was, the spat between the historians was of considerably less significance than the simmering dispute between Derby and its offspring, Ansonia. For a good many years Ansonians thought of the arrangement that placed them in the town of Derby as a case of the tail wagging the dog. Ansonia had more than 10,000 residents, while the rest of Derby had fewer than 6,000. Ansonia also had factories employing more than 2,000 workers and it seemed to Anso-

The shore of what is known as the Long Island Sound has been a magnet for its fishing, clamming, and bathing opportunities for hundreds of years. The people gathering clams here on Milford Beach in the late 1800s were simply repeating what the Native Americans had done for centuries, although with less need to dry and store for trade. Courtesy, Dorothy Tanner

M.D., led to a falling out of the authors. Shortly after the book appeared, Orcutt in a letter to the editor of the *Journal*, complained about the use of the word "Ousatonic" in the book. He said the evidence suggested that "Housatonic" was more correct and noted that the use of "Ousatonic" was a source of "decided mortification to me." He signed the letter, "Samuel Orcutt,

nians that the taxes from these plants were always being used to pay for public works that mainly benefited the rest of Derby.

Thus it was that in November 1888 a petition signed by 1,100 Ansonia residents was submitted to the General Assembly, seeking town status for Ansonia. The petition was opposed vigorously in the legislature by the people of Derby and Birmingham. So in-

tense was the struggle that a public hearing on the question extended over three days so that all the witnesses could be heard.

Finally, after a good deal of parliamentary maneuvering, the bill was voted out of committee. The Senate approved the division of Derby 17 to 3, the House went along 121 to 90, and the bill making Ansonia a town was signed into law on April 15, 1889.

Ironically, while politicians were dividing the Valley's people into separate towns, entrepreneurs continued to introduce machines that drew them closer together.

In November 1880 the *Transcript* reported, "At last Derby, Birmingham, Ansonia and Shelton are to be united in one telephone exchange, the central office to be located in the Birmingham Post Office in charge of Walter Sperry which insures competent management . . . The circuits will be immediately run to Ansonia which will give our friends there as good accommodations as if the central office was located there. Already 15 connections are in working order

LEFT: The first spike for Derby's new electric railway was struck on May 2, 1887, introducing a new era of transportation to the Naugatuck Valley. Completed one year later, the first passenger trolley in New England made its premiere run along the tracks that ran from Ansonia to Derby and back again. Construction workers are shown here in 1887, laying the tracks along Main Street in Ansonia. Courtesy, Derby Historical Society

FACING PAGE, TOP: In the 45 years since Anson Phelps purchased the Kinneytown Dam in Seymour and laid out a canal and reservoir to provide power for mills in the area now called Ansonia, the borough had grown sufficiently to petition the legislature for separate town status. Tremont Street and the factories lining the canal in the early 1890s bear witness to this growth. Courtesy, Derby Historical Society

FACING PAGE, BOTTOM: Many Naugatuck Valley senior citizens who grew up in Derby remember attending the "old" Irving School at the corner of Olivia and Fifth streets. Pictured here shortly after the separation of Ansonia from Derby in 1889, this building also served as the Birmingham High School from 1869 through 1906, until the community's new high school structure was built on Minerva Street. The school was eventually demolished in 1954 and is now the site of the Derby City Hall. Courtesy, Derby Public Library

and everything bids fair to give us what we have so long waited for, a first class telephone exchange."

A few years later the Derby electric street railroad, the first electric railroad in New England, drew Ansonia and Derby even closer. The railroad's debut was on May 1, 1888, when 30 guests were invited to make the run from Ansonia to Derby and back. The *New Haven Palladium*, among others, was quite impressed:

The motor was a handsome cream-colored four-wheeled car, sixteen feet in length and handsomely upholstered. About four feet of the forward end of the car is partitioned off and in the compartment is situated the motor of about three or four horsepower . . . The motor soon struck a grade in which was a rise of five feet in 100 and around a curve of 200 feet radius. It went very smoothly and nicely. When it came to Miller's place the rise was seven feet in 100, and the car was stopped so as to prove that it could be readily started again. The plan was entirely successful. Through Derby avenue a speed of 12 miles an hour was obtained and the trip down of three and three-quarters

miles was made in about twenty minutes . . .

Even the achievement of the electric railroad paled, however, in comparison to the dream of another Valley resident. In November 1896 Joseph Busoske of Derby, a mechanic at the Sterling Co. plant, twice hauled an apparatus with four-foot wings constructed of a light but strong framework, up on the railway trestle at the foot of Caroline Street and tried to fly. Each time he failed, landing unceremoniously in the mud and water under the trestle.

Some folks laughed at Busoske, but they were people who didn't have the sense to lift their eyes or their imaginations above the mud and water beneath the trestle. More thoughtful folks perhaps recalled how the iron horse had chugged into the Valley 50 years before, bringing with it a half-century of mind-boggling change and growth, and wondered whether this immigrant mechanic—"a mixture of Hungarian and Polander," the *Sentinel* called him—might not be a forerunner of marvelous things that lay ahead.

Patriotism was fanned by the country's participation in World War I, as men and women of all ethnic backgrounds in the Naugatuck Valley rallied to the colors in record numbers. This Memorial Day Parade in Ansonia honored those representing the town in the forces overseas. Courtesy, Derby Historical Society

A Beauty Never To Be Forgotten

T he 20th century," exulted the *Evening Sentinel* on January 1, 1901, "dawned in Ansonia with a beauty never to be forgotten by those who were out of doors to welcome it. After a day of damp and rain, a fitting pall for the dying year, the veil of clouds parted, leaving the heavens clear, still and grand in the moonlight. The night could not have been more beautiful."

The mood of the Valley matched the weather. Scots, Germans, and Lithuanians danced the night away at their clubs in Derby and Seymour, while across the Housatonic River in Shelton the Methodist Episcopal Church hosted an interdenominational service, where the Reverend E.O. Tree expressed the hope that the coming together of four congregations was a preview of the brotherhood that would characterize Valley life in the new century.

Valley folks got a more realistic preview of what the early years of the twentieth century held in store on January 2, when assemblers at the Williams Typewriter Co. in Derby went out on strike rather than take a cut in pay. The assemblers' strike was quickly settled, but two months later 70 women workers in the underwear-finishing room at the Paugussett Mills in Derby walked off the job in a labor dispute that was settled only through the personal intervention of the president of the American Federation of Labor. Fifty-four days after the strike began, Samuel Gompers came to Derby on Friday, May 10, went into a whirlwind round of meetings with the strikers and management, and by Saturday evening was able to announce to a capacity crowd at the Sterling Opera House that the strike had been settled.

The man who persuaded Gompers to intervene, Stephen Charters, president of the local carpenters union, was himself soon thrust into the limelight by another of the many labor disputes that ushered in the new century. On May 20, 1901, about 500 employees of the Farrel Foundry and Machinery Co. in Ansonia walked off their jobs when the company refused to grant them a pay increase and a nine-hour working day.

The strike continued into late July, the company hired replacement workers, and Charters was arrested on charges that he had conspired to intimidate one of the newcomers. A crowd of 1,000 union sympathizers pressed close around the sheriffs escorting Charters to the railroad station whence he was to be taken to jail in New Haven, and it was touch-and-go for a while whether an attempt would be made to free him.

Charters returned to Ansonia a town hero, and when the unions decided to nominate a labor candidate for mayor, the erstwhile conspirator was nominated on a fusion ticket of laboring men and Democrats and subsequently elected mayor of Ansonia. His election even attracted the notice of the New York City papers, the *Tribune* commenting that Charters "was borne into the mayor's office on the tidal wave of unionism."

Not all labor relations in the Valley were acrimonious. The Howe Pin Co. of Derby, for example, was a leader in giving workers a greater stake in their company's fortunes. In 1903 Howe initiated an employee bonus in which workers received at Christmastime the amount of the annual interest that would be earned on their salaries. "No wonder," commented the *Sentinel,* "that it is able to keep its employees for long terms of service and that labor disturbances are unknown within its precincts." The experiment, said the paper, would be "watched with interest in industrial circles in the Naugatuck Valley."

RIGHT: Stephen Charters, president of the local Derby carpenters union at the turn of the century, became a town hero as a result of his efforts on behalf of the workers during the 1901 strike at the Farrel Foundry and Machinery Company. This stand catapulted him into the position of Ansonia's mayor from 1901-1905, and then again from 1906-1912. Courtesy, Ansonia Public Library

BELOW: Shown here at his desk at the Birmingham Brass facility in Shelton around the turn of the century, John A. Coe survived all of the labor management negotiations at his company. He went on to become president of American Brass, a conglomerate of several Naugatuck Valley brass companies. Courtesy, Derby Historical Society

Another kind of experiment being watched closely in the Valley, as elsewhere, was the horseless carriage. The same year that Howe introduced its profit-sharing plan, Connecticut began issuing license plates for cars. Connecticut license plate No. 7 was issued to Norwood Hall of Ansonia. Charles B. Brewster of Derby got the first license plate in that town, No. 36. Louise B. Crofut, also of Derby, was among the first women in the state to secure a license plate, hers bearing the number 306. William N. Smith got Shelton's first plate, No. 439; F.H. Beecher was the first in Seymour with No. 526; and Homer D. Bronson, with plate No. 1207, was the first in Beacon Falls. No one in Oxford was granted a license during the first year of registration.

Some horses—and their masters—fought back. One warm evening in May 1903, Derby resident Herman Schultz got into a shouting match with a couple of motorists whose automobiles were blocking his horse from drinking at the watering trough on Wakelee Avenue. The motorists had Schultz arrested for cursing them out, and the next morning the horseman was found guilty of using abusive language and ordered to pay $10 and costs.

Other Valley folks saw the horseless carriage as an opportunity rather than an

enemy. D.H. Riggs and some other Seymour entrepreneurs established one of the area's first motorized transit systems, the Auto Express Co. They advertised that their Locomobile would make a daily morning trip to New Haven, averaging 25 miles per hour. In the afternoon the vehicle would be used to deliver packages about town.

And an Italian immigrant, Giovanni Lombardi, gave up his bicycle sales and repair business on Elizabeth Street in Derby and established one of the first service stations and car dealerships in the Valley. His success story was mirrored by those of thousands of other immigrants pouring into the Valley. They came from the four corners of the earth and they came wave upon wave right up to mid-century. By 1930 almost 25 percent of all Valley residents were foreign-born. Of the 49,382 people in Ansonia, Beacon Falls, Derby, Seymour, and Shelton at that time, 13,219 were foreign-born, and that doesn't even include the thousands of others who were children of immigrants.

Italian and Polish immigrants predominated, but there were also natives of Russia, Lithuania, Austria, Germany, Canada, Sweden, Czechoslovakia, Greece, Hungary, and a galaxy of other nations. Even the Orient was represented, for in the early years of the century, two Chinese, Quong Sing and Wang Lee, established laundries on Main Street in Ansonia.

The immigrants clung together in ghettoes like Derby's "Battle Row," a Polish enclave of shanties and flats along the Housatonic River. The men worked in the mills and paid $8 to $13 a month to rent shanties or flats above stores. "But everybody helped each other," recalled Raymond Skowronski in a 1980 newspaper account of Battle Row. "There was a woman midwife who came in to help the women have their babies . . . And the farmers would come down at night to bring the vegetables they didn't sell that day and our mothers would pay half-price."

The mingling of so many peoples certainly made Valley life lively. Some ethnic group was always petitioning for something. In October 1909, for example, officials of the Greek Catholic Ss. Peter and Paul Church petitioned that the name of May Street in Ansonia be changed to Chmelnyzky Street in honor of a fifteenth century Russian general. "It will be harder for the average Ansonia citizen to pronounce Chmelnyzky than to say May," conceded the *Sentinel*. "The people of St. Peter and St. Paul parish believe, however, that everyone will be able to say Chmelnyzky in a short time . . . Would not most people, they ask, rather say Chmelnysky than Apalachchicola , Tuscaloosa, Mishawaka, Oklaloosa or Ottumwa . . . ?"

The same week the barbers of Derby and Shelton were signing a petition to close on Columbus Day. "Most of the journeymen in this city," commented the *Sentinel*, "are Italians and would be especially pleased to have this day off."

All this ferment was a bit alarming to old-line Valley folks. One of them, the Reverend F.A. Holden, pastor of the Huntington Congregational Church in Shelton, wrote, "Our whole attitude toward the immigrant should change. If we knew him better, we should cease to despise him. The men and women who have the energy and ambi-

tion to leave the old home in a far off land and come here may be poor and dirty and ignorant, but they are, a large proportion of them, good material to work on and are worthy of our respect and we should try to help them and their children to become good Americans."

Some Valley residents did hold out helping hands to the foreigners. Sarah Riggs Humphreys' chapter of the Daughters of the American Revolution, for example, printed abstracts of Connecticut laws in Italian and Polish and distributed them to foreigners, and purchased books in Yiddish and other languages and donated them to the Derby Public Library.

The immigrants reciprocated by enriching Valley life with their cultures. In 1912 the Concordia Singing Society entertained residents of Seymour with a five-act German play which, said the *Sentinel*, "held the close attention of all until the final curtain fell." And when the Italians of Ansonia sponsored an outdoor concert byTrapano's Savoia Band of New Haven, nearly 1,000 residents of all nationalities turned out to enjoy international music.

The advent of the automobile created quite a stir in the Naugatuck Valley, and a drive in this new "horseless carriage" was a local event. On an outing in 1904 in their Pierce Stanhope, the Pages were photographed by their unidentified companion while stopped along River Road in Shelton. Mr. Page is visible to the rear of the vehicle, making some minor adjustments as his wife looks on. Courtesy, Derby Historical Society

Many Lower Naugatuck Valley churches served specific ethnic congregations. St. Mary's, which served a predominantly Irish congregation at the turn of the century, saw its ranks enlarged by the new Italian and Polish population. Here, the congregation has gathered to celebrate the laying of the convent cornerstone, under the direction of Father Charles J. McElroy. Courtesy, Derby Public Library

Any lingering doubts about the patriotism of the newcomers were dispelled by their response to American entry into World War I, for Valley men and women of all ethnic backgrounds rallied to the colors in record numbers. By August 1918 E.J. Fitzpatrick, who was inscribing the names of Ansonia soldiers on the town's large outdoor honor roll, reported that he was running out of room. Fitzpatrick said he was only on the "P's" and had already recorded 730 names. He estimated he had another 400 names to go, and town officials worried whether there would be space enough on the honor roll if another draft was carried out.

As willingly as they went off to fight,

however, men and women in the armed forces still longed for the Valley. In a letter to a friend, Emil J. Fournier of the 102nd Infantry commented, "France might be some place, but when this war is over and I am still living, little Ansonia will be good enough for me."

Back in "little Ansonia" and the other Valley towns, factories could scarcely find enough workers to turn out all the war orders. A government employment bureau was set up in the old YMCA building on Elizabeth Street in Derby to direct the distribution of labor throughout the Valley. William Bowen, supervisor of the bureau, estimated that 800 skilled workers could be put on the job immediately. "Every woman who can be spared from the home life has a niche ready for her in some factory in this locality," reported the *Sentinel*, adding that a special recruiting committee was getting in touch with every potential worker to "impress upon him or her the need for service."

The war fanned patriotism to fever pitch and when it ended, "Americanization" became the order of the day. In May 1919 the Americanization committee in Derby and Shelton began classes to make sure that the estimated 2,000 to 2,500 foreigners who worked in Valley factories spoke English. Comcowich Post, Veterans of Foreign Wars, went so far as to adopt a resolution opposing publication of foreign language newspapers "as an act of disloyalty" to the United States.

The motivation behind the Americanization programs was the fear of communism, and during the infamous Red Scare, federal agents descended upon the Valley and arrested dozens of supposed communists.

The first raid took place on November 7, 1919, when, as part of a nationwide dragnet, nearly two score alleged radicals were arrested in Ansonia, many of them taken at a hall on Maple Street that was reportedly the headquarters of Valley radicals. Taken with them, reported the *Sentinel*, was "a truck load of books, papers and other things . . . Framed and unframed pictures of Lenin and Trotsky, the Russian Bolshevik leaders, and red flags . . . "

The roundup of radicals continued in early January when 30 more Ansonia residents, along with five Seymour residents, two men from Derby, and one from Shelton, were arrested. More suspects were captured in Ansonia than in any other town in the state.

If radicals were losing some political freedoms during this time, however, women were gaining some. In November 1920, thanks to the 19th Amendment to the U.S. Constitution, Valley women got their first chance to vote in a presidential election. In Shelton, said the *Sentinel*, "quite a number of women became confused and incorrectly

The family of Dominick LaMacchia of Shelton was part of the vast immigration wave that occurred in the country between 1870 and 1910. Determined to make good in the "Land of Opportunity," they worked hard, took pride in their accomplishments, and kept the local photographers busy with the family portraits that documented their success. Courtesy, the LaMacchia Family

marked their ballots, but returned them to the ticket distributors and received new ones. The fact that [both] men and women voted added considerable interest to the election and throngs of people were about the streets all day discussing and predicting on the probable outcome."

Valley residents also threw themselves ardently into the cause of political freedom for their overseas kinsmen. Jews in both Ansonia and Derby organized committees to promote the cause of Zionism. And Ansonia's Irish went $1,500 over their goal of $5,000 when they conducted a citywide canvass in 1921 to raise funds for the cause of Irish independence.

Another eminently successful fund-raising drive was that conducted for the expansion of Derby's Griffin Hospital, which had opened its doors in 1909. In 1924 residents of Ansonia, Derby, Shelton, and Seymour raised $179,666 for a maternity wing and nursing school at the facility.

Amid such serious projects Valley folks still found time to relax with one of their first loves—sports. Ansonia was home to not only a highly regarded professional basketball team, which played such top-flight squads as the New York Knickerbockers, but also a

football team that won national acclaim. In 1921 the Ansonia High School gridders went undefeated in the regular season, whipped Elgin, Illinois, High School in a special post-season game, and enjoyed a trip to Washington, D.C., and an interview with President Harding. The Yale crew races on Lake Housatonic, the lake formed by the damming of the Housatonic River, were a major spectator sport. The races drew upwards of 10,000 spectators, many of them arriving on special excursion trains and lining both the Shelton and Derby sides of the lake.

Movies, too, were all the rage, and Ansonia's Capitol Theater drew large crowds, creating an entirely new type of problem. "Something will have to be done," stated the *Sentinel*, "to clear Main Street of the motor vehicles . . . Numbers of New Haven people visit Ansonia once or twice a week to attend the show at the Capitol Theater . . . and together with people who come from Derby, Shelton, Seymour and Beacon Falls in automobiles, it will be a question where to put all of the cars."

After 1929, Valley people had more serious problems than parking. A survey completed by the Storrs Agricultural Experiment Station in 1934 showed that during the first four years of the Great Depression, Valley towns lost 2,335 jobs in manufacturing alone. Describing the plight of the estimated 7,000 Valley people on relief, the survey stated:

Many houses originally designed for one family dwellings have become quarters for two, three and four families with no regard for privacy or safety . . . In some families, as many as five half-grown children are forced to sleep in one bed; in other cases families of 12 and 13 live in four rooms . . . Running water is available in most of the houses, but almost none of them have provisions for running hot water. Where electric meters have been turned off for economy or for failure to pay back bills, kerosene lamps and candles are used for illumination . . . Because of the expense, most of the

Pride and respect for the nation were especially intense prior to the onset of World War I. School portraits were taken in front of the American flag, and Maude Boone, pictured here circa 1910, remembers the day when the photographer came to the Holbrook Street School. Courtesy, the Boone Family

poor families do not seek medical attention except in acute cases . . .

Local charities did what they could, but it wasn't nearly enough. In January 1933 Ethel Ericson, secretary of the Derby Relief Fund, reported that 500 pairs of shoes were needed immediately. "It is a terrible thing," she said, "to turn people away when their feet are on the ground."

In Shelton, Mutual Aid, Inc. established a reading room in a vacant storefront because, it said, "So many unemployed men find home a confining place day after day. Park benches are inhospitable in this kind of weather and street corners are even worse. The meeting and exchanging of opinions, friendly games and a warm place to read and discuss the day's news will do much to lift the gloom from many men's minds."

Women were in many cases worse off than men because all the relief efforts were directed toward those presumed to be the breadwinners for families. The *Sentinel* in December 1933 cited a number of cases of women left to fend for themselves by the Depression. "Within this very community," it said, "there are to be found dozens of them who have exhausted every avenue of approach for work and who are still without employment or any hope of employment."

That same year, however, the Roosevelt Administration's recovery programs

began to make an impact. The National Industrial Recovery Act program came to the Valley with great fanfare. In Ansonia a parade preceded a mass meeting where speakers from every sector of the community appealed for cooperation. The meeting was followed by a campaign to get business, industry, workers, and consumers to sign cards pledging to live by codes agreed upon by labor and management.

New Deal programs did make a difference. In Seymour the Civil Works Administration put 110 people to work on road and park projects. In Ansonia 1,343 men were employed, and by late 1935 public works projects in Derby alone included: refurbishing of cemeteries, renovation of the interiors and exteriors of schools and the public library, construction of a road on Sentinel Hill, improvement of Chatfield Road, construction of a municipal park, draining of swamps along the Naugatuck River, cleaning out of apple maggots and gypsy moths, and renovation of City Hall.

Meanwhile, the private sector was busy too. The Derby-Shelton Board of Trade began a campaign to attract new industry to the

ABOVE: The men of the Valley rallied to their country's call during World War I. These local boys trained at the Newport, Rhode Island, naval station in July 1917. Seated from left to right are Anthony Donato, Fred Nichols, and Sam Swirsky; standing from left to right are Alfred Thurston, young Hopkins, Henry Conklin, and Vincent Impellitteri. Courtesy, Rose Comcowich

LEFT: Opened in 1909, the Griffin Hospital in Derby is pictured here prior to its 1924 expansion. The original structure is located to the right of the arched windows. The central and left sections were added in 1915 to make room for an additional 24 patients, a new laundry facility, and new nurses' quarters. This entire building was demolished to make way for the East Wing of the present Griffin Hospital, which was completed in 1968. Courtesy, Charles Rotteck

Valley, and by 1936 *Connecticut Industry* magazine carried a headline boasting, perhaps a bit optimistically, "Depression whipped in Derby and Shelton." The magazine told how the Board of Trade's campaign had paid off by putting hundreds of Valley people back to work and increasing payrolls in Valley towns by nearly $1million a year.

Even as the domestic situation improved, however, America was drawn toward the whirlpool of war already engulfing much of the rest of the world. On Sunday, December 7, 1941, while the combined choirs of the Methodist congregations in Ansonia and Seymour were rehearsing for their presentation of Handel's *Messiah*, and the Ukrainian Youth Organization was conducting its fifth annual convention in Liberty Hall in Ansonia, Valley residents heard on their radios the first fragmented reports of a Japanese attack on Pearl Harbor.

Within weeks the heavy industries of the Valley were gearing up for war production. At the Seymour Manufacturing Co., reported *Connecticut Circle* magazine, "Long lines of up-to-the-minute electric furnaces supply molten metal day and night, batteries of rolls reduce it to sheet and presses up to 500 tons blank out discs to be made into shell casings." The Seymour Products Co. switched from making suitcase hardware to turning out military hardware. Production

soared to seven times peacetime levels, and women soon accounted for 60 percent of the work force. Farrel-Birmingham was turning out propulsion gears for ships, molds for gun barrels, and hydraulic presses for forming airplane parts. Chemists at the Sponge Rubber Co. in Shelton developed a product made of 100 percent reclaimed rubber and got the green light from the War Production Board to begin manufacturing padding for jeeps and tanks.

If the 24-hour-a-day operations at local factories didn't bring the war home to Valley people, the *Sentinel* did on Monday, February 2, 1942, when it reported the first battle casualty: Marine Private Warren Carver killed, the War Department said, "somewhere in the Pacific."

Two weeks later 3,170 men between

the ages of 20 and 45 signed up at the first draft registration in Valley towns: 1,450 in Ansonia, 603 in Shelton, 542 in Derby, 392 in Seymour, 120 in Beacon Falls, and 63 in Oxford.

Within a year Valley men and women were serving quite literally in the four corners of the earth. Army Sergeant Evo Bracci of Derby was in Iran building a supply road from the Persian Gulf to the Soviet Union. On the South Pacific island of New Britain, a Shelton boy, Staff Sergeant Michael Churma, a chef, ran what came to be known as "Churma's Hot Springs Cafe" on the road to Rabaul. Seaman Angelo Marasco of Seymour, in peacetime the orchestra leader on a luxury liner, logged 286,000 miles serving on troopships in almost every theater of war and meeting up with 372 Valley soldiers in the process.

On the beach at Anzio, Private John Comcowich of Shelton jumped into a foxhole and found a copy of *The Evening Sentinel*, left there, he subsequently learned, by John Tiano, a Derby GI also serving in Italy. In the Pacific, Radioman Third Class Henry Healey of Derby and Seaman Vincent DeCapua of Shelton clambored aboard a lifeboat sent to rescue them when their destroyer, the *Porter*, was sunk. They were greeted by one of the lifeboat's crew, Fireman Vito Voccia of Derby.

On D-Day, June 6, 1944, Seaman Robert Gavin of Derby was on the destroyer *Herndon* as it led the invasion forces at Normandy; while Air Corps Sergeant Clarence Hubbell of Oxford wrote his family, "The day the world has been waiting for has come and will be remembered for centuries to come. Entire crew and plane in A-1 shape . . . " That same day PFC Charles Emerson, a Derby paratrooper, was killed after landing behind German lines, but not before he and two other GIs had held up an enemy counterattack for an hour and a half, giving the rest of his unit time to form a defensive line, an act for which he was posthumously awarded the Silver Star.

In an all-out effort to offset the pending invasion of their country, Japanese pilots began a campaign of suicide strikes against American ships. One such Kamikaze pilot slammed into a vulnerable area of the destroyer Porter *in 1945, causing it to sink. Henry Healey of Derby, pictured here, who was one of the men aboard the destroyer, was found by fellow townsman Vito Voccia, a member of the rescue team. Courtesy, Henry Healey*

When the war finally ended, Gunner's Mate Michael Pawlak of Seymour was on board the destroyer *Buchanan* in Tokyo Bay. "This morning," he wrote on September 2, 1945, "the *Buchanan* had the honor of taking Gen. MacArthur and a lot of other big boys to the U.S. *Missouri* for the Jap surrender signature. We went to Yokohama naval base to pick them up . . . The *Buchanan* took aboard Gen. MacArthur, Gen. Hap Arnold, Jimmy Doolittle, Gen. Stilwell and even Gen. Wainwright . . . Oh yes, aboard our ship was the Russian general, Zhukov."

Another Seymour man in Japan at the time of the surrender was PFC Joseph Kriz of the 1st Cavalry Division. The division was one of the first units to enter Japan. In a letter home, Kriz wrote, "We made the landing here in boats like the ones you see in the movies, 1,400 men hitting the shore at once. First though, about a thousand planes went on a convoy all set to drop bombs if anything started. I chewed three plugs of tobacco . . . while we were waiting to go in . . . "

Kriz closed his letter expressing what was probably on the minds of most Valley folks, whether at home or abroad, that day: "I'll certainly be a peaceable man after all this fighting . . . "

Just two months after the first electric trolley completed its run, the world's first electric freight locomotive made its debut along the same route on July 2, 1888. It transported industrial freight from Ansonia to the Naugatuck Valley Steamboat Company wharf, where goods were then shipped to Pier 39 on New York's East River. In celebration of its 100th anniversary, the locomotive was returned to the Naugatuck Valley from the Branford Trolley Museum for festivities and a historic running of its original route. Courtesy, United Illuminating Company

Some Things Old, Some Things New

Those who live in the Lower Naugatuck Valley have never been strangers to flooding. More than 200 years ago, the *Connecticut Gazette* reported on February 7, 1767, that Joseph Hawkins had lost "a large white pine canoe" when a January thaw and a day of rain caused the Naugatuck River to flood at Derby.

Eighty years later, on February 4, 1847, the *Derby Journal* reported, after another day of rain, "The waters of the Housatonic and Naugatuck rivers began to swell, inundating the meadows and lowlands along their banks . . . Soon the causeway connecting this village [Birmingham] with Derby was overflowed . . . From our office windows could be seen one broad expanse of water while the continued passing and repassing of boats in pursuit of floating property or the conveyance of passengers from one side to the other gave a sort of novelty to the occasion that is not often witnessed."

An even more exciting scene occurred 44 years later, on January 21, 1891, when after another day of rain, melting snow, and high winds, the Ousatonic Dam collapsed. "The grandeur of the scene at the dam during this work of destruction is indescribable," said the *Evening Sentinel*. "The waters were awful to behold and as they came down the river in one wild rush, bringing with them monstrous cakes of ice and flinging these with terrific force against the walls of the dam, they seemed like some demon bent on pulling down entire the whole solid wall of masonry. And when once they did make an opening in the wall stone after stone was picked up and plunged over into the water below like it was without weight."

Such scenes have been repeated for more than three centuries in the Valley, but even an area so accustomed to floods was not prepared for what happened on August 19,

1955—Black Friday to Valley residents. Earlier that month the tail end of Hurricane Connie had swept through Connecticut, soaking the ground with nine inches of rain. On Wednesday, August 17, another heavy rain drenched the Valley. Then beginning on the morning of August 18, the northern edge of Hurricane Diane—ironically downgraded to a tropical storm as it moved northward along the Atlantic Coast—struck the Valley. Six inches of rain fell in Ansonia, eight inches in Naugatuck, 10 inches in Waterbury, and 12 inches in Thomaston. That much water pouring into the deep, narrow Valley already saturated from previous rains guaranteed a disaster.

By 4 a.m. Friday, August 19, a terrible floodtide was roaring down the Valley. Many Valley residents, accustomed as they were to periodic flooding, went about their business. Mrs. John Navarro said she "did not think it was going to be a flood and did not pay much attention to it" when she noticed water accumulating in the backyard of her home at 34 Caroline Street in Derby about 8:30 a.m. Two hours later the water was flooding her cellar and coming up through the kitchen floor. She bundled up her five children and went to the upper story of her house where she was later rescued.

The power station in Ansonia was soon flooded and the city was without electricity, while 8,000 telephones in Ansonia, Derby, and Seymour were also out of service. Ansonia streets rapidly became part of the angry Naugatuck River, the racing waters swirling ever higher on cars and parking meters, smashing in the doors and windows of stores and carrying away everything from lumber to barrels of cod-liver oil.

In Seymour huge slabs of concrete from Route 8 were tossed about like corks on the floodtide. The north wall of Seymour High School was caved in and the auditorium and gymnasium battered. A famous Seymour restaurant, the Dutch Door Inn, stood on a little peninsula jutting out into the river, reached by an old iron bridge. The raging waters carried away the inn, the bridge, and the peninsula too.

Mobile homes floated down the river to Seymour from Beacon Falls, and caskets

The combined forces of the rushing water and the pounding of the ice smashed into the solid wall of masonry on the eastern side of the Ousatonic Dam on January 21, 1891, causing its collapse. Large chunks simply broke off the dam, and pieces of granite as large as a man lay strewn along the shore. Courtesy, Derby Historical Society

uprooted from the Union Cemetery in Seymour floated down the river to Derby. "It was like the end of the world," recalled Nicholas Martino of Ansonia. "There were corpses in flowing white robes in the river."

In Ansonia the American Brass Co. bridge, torn from its foundation and tossed about like a toy, smashed into an eight-family tenement called the Vartelas Block. The block trembled, said an observer, "like a man grabbed by the neck and shaken." The structure swayed momentarily; then its east wall and roof fell into the river and were swept downstream, remaining intact until they hit another bridge and splintered into smithereens. Residents of the block were evacuated just minutes before it was hit.

One of those evacuating them was Peter Waniga, proprietor of a package store on Maple Street. Waniga loaded people into his brand-new 1955 Ford station wagon and drove them to safety across the Maple Street

Bridge. As he was driving back across the bridge, it was struck by a portion of the brass company bridge. Waniga leaped from his vehicle and scrambled to safety just in time to watch the Maple Street span collapse, taking his station wagon with it.

The roofs of Ansonia buildings became rescue stations. When a National Guard truck carrying a dozen evacuees stalled at Water and Canal streets, the people were led through a laundry and a tenement up onto the roof of the Capitol Theater, where they were eventually rescued by helicopter. People from the roof of the Arlington Hotel were also rescued by helicopter. One of those rescued, Maurice Karlins, recalled, "The pilot had to maneuver down to the slanted roof and set one wheel on the steep pitch. Then one of his crew reached down and helped haul us in, one after the other . . . We finally made it and were down in the Farrel parking lot. We all prayed."

Hundreds were evacuated by boat and by human chains, and dozens were rescued by the heroic efforts of firemen, policemen, and volunteers. Anthony Ziomek of the Derby Police Department stripped off his clothes and dove into the swollen river to rescue a woman being carried away by the current.

George O'Donnell of Derby's Storm Engine Co. was trying to rescue two elderly people on Factory Street when his boat was struck by a submerged object and he was thrown out into the raging water. He bounced off the side of an overturned truck, smashed into a car, clung momentarily to a no-parking sign, and was unconscious by the time he was finally rescued from the top of a tree.

Robert DiMauro rescued 20 children stranded in a building on Water Street in Ansonia, one of them an infant whom he held high over his head while threading his way across Main Street. DiMauro had just handed the baby to other rescuers when he was struck by a bathtub being carried along by the tide. His ribs broken, DiMauro was carried four blocks by the river until someone threw the end of a blanket out a window and yelled to him to hold on. He was pulled to safety through the window into the upper story of a building.

The Naugatuck, whose average depth was two feet, crested at Ansonia that day at 23 feet, nine feet above its previously recorded high. It was, the experts said, a 400-year storm, a storm so intense that it would occur only once in 400 years. The storm took 100 lives but, miraculously, only two in the lower Valley—two Seymour women who refused the appeals of rescuers to leave their homes.

Property losses were staggering. For the six towns in the lower Valley, damage was put at $23.7 million. Ansonia suffered most: $14 million in damages, half of that to its industrial plants. Seymour suffered $6.5 million in damages; Beacon Falls, $2.3 million; Shelton, $612,000; Derby, $165,000; Oxford, $2,000.

Nearly 1,000 homes were damaged; factories lay in shambles, their machinery buried in silt and mud; bridges were destroyed; power lines were down; sewer, water, and gas lines were ruptured. The week after the flood, unemployment claims in Ansonia, Derby, and Seymour jumped from 629 to 5,000. It was truly the worst disaster in the

300-year history of the Valley. And to make matters worse, scarcely had the Valley completed the massive cleanup than another flood struck on October 15 and 16.

Still, folks whose roots were in the Valley wasted little time bemoaning their luck. Ansonia Mayor Joseph Doyle went off to Washington to lobby for flood control assistance and returned with a promise of $20 million.

Over the next 15 years the Army Corps

BELOW: Reconstruction of the Ousatonic Dam, following the January 1891 collapse, began in March of that same year. Designer D.S. Brinsmade introduced a sloping apron to allow water to sweep down with "almost silent grace," to avoid another washout caused by the previous vertical design. Courtesy, Derby Public Library

LEFT: As Peter Waniga was crossing the Maple Street Bridge while returning from his last rescue attempt on August 19, 1955, a section of the American Brass bridge struck the Maple Street Bridge and sent it into the swirling waters. Leaping from his station wagon, which was left precariously abandoned on the far side of the bridge, Waniga scrambled to safety just in time to watch the final moments of the bridge's collapse. Courtesy, Derby Historical Society

of Engineers used that money in Ansonia to straighten 7,400 feet of river channel and to build 10,400 feet of earthen dikes and 6,700 feet of concrete floodwalls. Up and down the Valley new dams and embankments were constructed, at a cost of $70 million, until the Naugatuck watershed was the best protected region in the entire state.

Meanwhile, redevelopment went on apace. With almost $43 million in federal aid, Ansonia built a shopping mall in its blighted downtown, constructed 100 homes, rebuilt upper Main Street, and replaced decaying houses on Liberty Street.

While Ansonia was pulling itself up by its bootstraps, Shelton was struck by yet another disaster. In 1974 the B.F. Goodrich Co. announced it would close its Sponge Rubber Co., an old two-and-one-half block factory on the Housatonic River in downtown Shelton. At the last moment the plant, where more than 1,000 workers were employed

making foam mattresses and pillows, was saved when Charles Moeller, an Ohio industrialist, bought it. Moeller was unable to turn the company's financial situation around, however, and in late 1974 his friend and spiritual adviser, a Tennessee minister, the Reverend David Bubar, began to plan a way out for Moeller.

Bubar hired a gang of Pennsylvania arsonists who arrived in the Valley in a rented truck filled with explosives. On the night of March 1, 1975, the arsonists gained entry to the plant by posing as telephone repairmen, kidnapped three security guards and dropped them off in a parking lot in the town of Monroe, set 2,000 feet of detonating cord and blew the plant up in the most awesome explosion in the history of the Valley—and probably in the history of the state.

The blast at 11:30 p.m. was felt miles away. It hurled 4,000-pound machines around and shattered concrete walls and

ABOVE: The Brownson Country Club Golf Course is one of the most popular spots for golfers in the Lower Naugatuck Valley. Named for Harry Brownson, on whose Shelton land the course is now located, the club hosts numerous Valley tournaments. Courtesy, Lower Naugatuck Valley Chamber of Commerce

FAR LEFT: This red colonial home in the Quaker Farms area is characteristic of eighteenth-century homes in Oxford. Settled in the late 1600s, much of this area remains rural today, although modern development is beginning to encroach upon the countryside. Courtesy, Lower Naugatuck Valley Chamber of Commerce

ABOVE: Built in 1893 and restored in 1985, Shelton's Pierpont Block on Howe Avenue is named for well-known financier J. Pierpont Morgan. Morgan's agent purchased this land when the railroad came to Shelton in 1888. The building today houses apartments, office facilities, and restaurant space. Photo by John Cessna

ABOVE: Holiday shoppers come from as far away as New York City to choose that special Christmas tree from Jones' Tree Farm in Shelton. Courtesy, Lower Naugatuck Valley Chamber of Commerce

RIGHT: The Osborne Homestead Museum in Derby is the former estate of Frances Osborne-Kellogg, businesswoman and philanthropist. An elegant 1850 Colonial Revival home adjacent to Osborne-dale State Park, the museum features the Osborne family's art and antique collection and a formal rose garden. Courtesy, Osborne Homestead Museum

The merry-go-round is a favorite ride for young and old alike at the Oxford Olde Tyme Fair, held each year during the last weekend in August on the grounds of Center School. Farm-fresh produce, craft displays, and live entertainment are all a part of this cherished summertime festival. Photo by John Cessna

ABOVE: The recently completed Kellogg Environmental Center in Derby is a central focus for environmental studies of the Lower Naugatuck Valley region, as well as for visiting state groups. A number of guided tours and classes are available at this extensive facility. Photo by John Cessna

FAR RIGHT: Located at the heart of the Bernard H. Matthies Memorial Park in Beacon Falls is this tranquil, romantic lake. The park's central island features the former family weekend retreat of Bernard and Ethel Clark Matthies. Although Matthies was a native of Seymour, his wife hailed from Beacon Falls, and the land on which the park now stands was donated to the town of Beacon Falls by Matthies in honor of his wife's heritage. Photo by John Cessna

ABOVE: This Derby Silver Company coffee and tea service, owned by Tina and Stephen Kobasa of Seymour, is exceptional because of its completeness. Pieces of Derby Silver are scarce today and are generally found only as individual items. The Kobasas have long been collectors of the company's wares. Photo by John Cessna

ABOVE: Evening concerts on the Huntington Green attract music lovers of all ages. Sponsored by area corporations and businesses, these festive gatherings are held every Wednesday during the summer months. Photo by John Cessna

RIGHT: This pristine view of the majestic Housatonic River above Indian Wells State Park includes the shores of Seymour, Derby, and Shelton, recalling the time when Indians first walked the land. Photo by John Cessna

windows along Canal Street. The FBI later called it the largest peacetime bombing in the history of the nation. Nearly 650 firefighters from 13 communities fought the fire, which raged until 7 a.m. the next morning. More than 3 million gallons of water were pumped from the river and an adjacent canal.

Bubar and nine others were convicted on various charges relating to the fire, while Moeller was acquitted of charges that he ordered the arson.

Meanwhile, more than 1,000 Valley people had been thrown out of work, many of them with years of seniority at the Sponge Rubber plant and with families to support. Some were able to capitalize on their skills. Stephen Kordiak and William Coffee founded Latex Foam Products, Inc., and began manufacturing pillows in 1977. Others took advantage of a job-training program established at Shelton High School after the disaster. Still others had to content themselves with part-time work and partial retirement.

The sad truth was, however, that if it hadn't gone up in flames, the Sponge Rub-

ber Co. was probably doomed anyway, a victim of the times. Up and down the Valley the heavy industries that clung to the river banks where they originally obtained water power were dying out, much less spectacularly but just as surely as the Sponge Rubber Co. In the years after World War II, manufacturing employment declined nearly 9 percent in the Valley. The flood of '55 aggravated the trend, and the Sponge Rubber fire seemed to be the last straw. Unemployment in the Valley rose well above 10 percent and remained that way, standing at 17 percent in the early 1980s.

Yet even while one door was being closed, another was being opened. As early as 1961 a planning report had noted a couple of favorable omens for the future of the Valley: New express highways were making the area more accessible, and New York City firms were beginning to relocate beyond New York suburbs.

During the 1970s and early 1980s, Route 8, which ran up along the Naugatuck River, was rebuilt as a modern superhighway, linking the Valley with Interstate 84 at Water-

The north-south artery of Route 8, which followed the original Indian trail along the Naugatuck River, was rebuilt as a superhighway after the flood of 1955. Construction of this structure at the intersection of Route 8 and Route 67 in Seymour is pictured here in the late 1950s. As a result of this new transportation corridor, housing developments were being chiseled out of forested hillsides, and new industrial parks were attracting new businesses by the 1980s. Courtesy, Citizen Engine Company, Seymour

The Lower Naugatuck Valley's mania for football has produced a standard of excellence unequaled in the state. On the way to its tenth state division championship in fourteen years, Ansonia High's defensive line is shown here battling against its archenemy Derby during the 1989 season. Ansonia's first line defense in this season limited opponents to less than three points per game. Courtesy, Ansonia High School

bury on the north and with Interstate 95 at Bridgeport on the south. Together with the completion in 1969 of the $3-million Oxford Airport with its 5,500-foot runway, the construction of the highway opened up the Valley to the high-tech industrial era that was dawning.

Shelton was in an ideal position to take advantage of this second industrial revolution. Situated astride the new Route 8, adjacent to Fairfield County's Gold Coast towns where New York firms began to locate in the 1960s and 1970s, and with 31 square miles of land area, it drew industrial developers like honey attracts bears.

By 1980 Shelton's tax list had been fattened by the arrival of such firms as Philips Medical Systems, ITT, Branson Cleaning Equipment, Nitsuko America Corp., and Richardson-Merrell. A total of 1,800 new jobs had already been created and there seemed to be no end to the expansion: Stauffer Chemical Co., Cartier, Inc., Paradyne Corp., Tetley Tea, Data Switch.

Seymour, too, shared in the new high-tech prosperity. To its Silvermine and Hubbell industrial parks, both situated on a ridge looking down on the Valley where industry originally flourished, came such firms as TIE Communications, Inc., Summagraphics, Inc., Plastic Molding Technology, and E.H. Emery.

At the end of the 1980s the Valley

Regional Planning Agency reported that employment in Shelton had increased 47 percent during the decade, with 4,290 jobs added, and employment in Seymour had grown by 34 percent with an increase of 1,000 jobs. The entire Valley shared in the prosperity, for by June 1988 unemployment throughout the area had been reduced to 2.6 percent, the lowest in a quarter of a century.

Even land-poor Derby and Ansonia were able to take advantage of the boom by jointly establishing the first two-city industrial park in the state. "We're really making history here today," Governor William A. O'Neill said on July 15, 1985, as he presided at the founding of the 120-acre Fountain Lake Commerce Park off the Wakelee Avenue exit of Route 8.

Such cooperative efforts have become a standard feature of Valley life. The founding of the Valley Association for Retarded Children and Adults in 1959 was followed by the formation of the Lower Naugatuck Valley Chamber of Commerce in 1964, the Valley Regional Planning Agency in 1966, and the Valley United Fund in 1968. In the latter year, Emmett O'Brien Regional Vocational Technical School, serving the entire Valley, was opened in Ansonia. And in 1971 one of the most successful regional efforts on a long-term basis began with the formation of the Valley Transit District's bus service.

The obvious benefits and savings of regional cooperation occasionally revive the dream some people have had for more than a century of consolidating what have come to be known as the "associated communities"—Ansonia, Derby, Shelton, Seymour, and Oxford. In the mid-nineteenth century an early consolidationist thought the communities should unite under the name "Urbs in Silva," or "City of the Woods"; while at the turn of the twentieth century, another thought it better to borrow a couple of letters from Derby, Ansonia, and Shelton, and call the new city "Deanshel." In the late 1960s state Republican Carl Ajello of Ansonia broached the question once again, suggesting that Birmingham might be a good name for the consolidated towns.

By whatever name, however, consolidation always stubs its toe on the rock of the fierce loyalty of Valley residents to their hometowns. A $25,000 study, conducted by the University of Connecticut's Institute for Public Service on Ajello's suggestion, held out the bright prospect of a unified city of 60 square miles and 75,000 people with a tax list of $350 million or more. It concluded, however, that selling the idea to tradition-bound Valley folks would be out of the question.

Strange as it may seem, not the least of the traditions that have kept the communities apart is their love affair with high school football. The Ansonia-Derby rivalry stretches back to 1902, and few residents of either town would give that up for the dubious advantages of consolidation. The Valley's football mania has produced a standard of excellence unequaled in Connecticut. In 1976 the state began a series of football playoffs leading to state championships. In the first 14 years of the playoffs, Ansonia High School won 10 state championships in the small-school division. Derby won one championship and finished as runner-up on three occasions, while Seymour and Shelton won one championship each.

Football, however, is by no means the only strong Valley tradition. Valley residents

Architecture designed in the style of a New England town and the characteristic rugged terrain of Beacon Falls make the Laurel Ledge elementary school a truly unique educational facility. Miss Amalavage's third-grade class is pictured here in front of the school's Tower building. Photo by John Cessna

take their historical traditions every bit as seriously. When the Huntington Green, where the Reverend Jedidiah Mills had greeted a messenger announcing the end of the French and Indian War, was threatened in 1979 by the request of a funeral home owner to rezone it for commercial use, outraged Shelton residents formed a Save the Green Committee and collected more than 1,000 signatures on petitions opposing the zone change.

When the Sterling Opera House in downtown Derby was threatened with demolition, the Sterling Opera House Foundation was formed to buy the 1889 landmark, where Houdini once fascinated audiences with his magic, and where John L. Sullivan performed equally impressive tricks with his fists. And when the pre-Civil War home of Dr. John Howe, who invented the machine that made the pin "common," was threatened by deteri-

Representatives of the Connecticut Fifth Regiment reenactment army prepare themselves for review in front of the Humphreys House in Ansonia on the 200th anniversary of the Yorktown Victory. Their American Revolution counterparts faced many a difficult hour in their determination to achieve freedom and independence the colonies. Photo by Cessna

oration, the Derby Historical Society sponsored a "Raising the Roof—We'll tell you Howe" campaign in which sponsors were asked to donate $25 per shingle to restore the tin shingle roof. The local efforts were matched by a $65,000 grant from the state, and the old home is being saved to become the Valley Industrial Museum.

Even as citizens were pulling out all stops to save the 1840s Howe house, a developer, S&S Enterprises, was planning to literally change the face of downtown Derby by razing a section of the south side of Main Street and building two 11-story apartment towers, 62,000 square feet of retail space, and 35,000 square feet of office

space along the riverfront behind it.

Thus, as the twentieth century draws to a close, the old and the new confront each other throughout the Valley, providing continual challenges to residents to preserve that which is time-honored, while yet welcoming progressive change.

In some cases ill-considered development has scarred the Valley. Yet in many instances a careful balance has been struck in which the old and the new mingle gracefully. Near the river bank in Beacon Falls, the four-story, red brick shops of the Home Woolen Co., built in 1853 and of sufficient importance to be listed on the National Register of Historic Places, have found new life as handsome apartment units. On the other side of the river, the one-room, 1779-vintage Rimmon Schoolhouse stands as a monument to the past—across Pinesbridge Road from the Ideal Manufacturing Co., where the business of the twentieth century is transacted.

In the Quaker Farms section of Oxford, the falls, which once produced power to run the machinery at the Diamond Match Co. factory, now serve as a beautiful backdrop for picnickers at Southford Falls State Park. Along North and South Cliff streets in Ansonia, stately nineteenth-century homes look down on the still-busy riverside factories of the Ansonia Copper and Brass Co. and the Farrel Co., where so many nineteenth-century immigrants got their start in America.

Indeed, were he once again to set out from New Haven, that venerable traveler Timothy Dwight might be as taken with the Lower Naugatuck Valley today as he was in 1811. Atop Academy Hill, where Josiah Holbrook and Truman Coe started one of the first vocational schools in the United States, he might pause by Brownie Castle, a saltbox home that itself has witnessed more than 300 years of Valley history since being built in 1686 by Samuel Bowers, son of the town's first minister.

Below him, and in the distance across the Valley, Dwight would see the symbols of religious faiths that play as important a role in the life of the Valley today as they did in Colonial times—the weathervaned steeple of Derby's First Congregational Church, the turreted top of St. James Episcopal Church on the Green in Derby, the soaring spire of St. Mary's Catholic Church, the newly sided Macedonia Baptist Church, the lofty Byzantine minarets and domes of Three Saints Orthodox Church, and Ss. Peter and Paul Ukrainian Catholic Church in Ansonia.

Along the riverbed he would catch glimpses of cars, trucks, and buses speeding along on the Valley's main artery, Route 8, a broad ribbon of concrete stretching off to the southwest, where glittering new office towers stand sentinel on the Shelton hills.

If he came in summertime, he would see thousands gathered at the Derby Day Festival, celebrating their ethnic diversity with everything from Italian and German foods to Spanish guitarists, Irish bagpipers, and Polish dancers. And if he came in autumn, he would see thousands gathered at Seymour's Pumpkin Festival or Oxford's Olde Tyme Fair, celebrating the harvest and renewing acquaintances much as the early settlers did at the agricultural fairs of yesteryear.

At almost anytime of the year, he would see old-timers strolling on Derby's pretty green and youngsters hiking the trails, first trod centuries ago by Native Americans,

in Indian Wells State Park in Shelton, at the Nature Center in Ansonia, and in the Naugatuck Forest in Beacon Falls. He would see summer cottages dotting the shores of Lake Housatonic and, farther up the river, the massive Stevenson Dam protecting the Valley against flood.

And it seems likely that when he completed his tour, propped himself up against a tree, and got out his pencil and paper to record what he had seen, Dwight might well begin with the very same words that he used nearly two centuries ago to describe the Lower Naugatuck Valley: "A rich and beautiful prospect."

The Ansonia Nature Center is a place of wonderment, where children can learn about local wildlife and gain a healthy respect for nature's creatures. Courtesy, Lower Naugatuck Valley Chamber of Commerce

The era of the horse-drawn carriage and trips to the local feed store would soon be a thing of the past with the advent of the horseless carriage. Some found the automobile to be more of an intrusion than a blessing. And indeed it was another step that removed people from the more natural and charming way of life evident in this scene on Howe Avenue in Shelton around the turn of the century. Courtesy, Derby Historical Society

Partners in Progress

The history of the Naugatuck Valley is a proud record of its people—friendly people who have put honest business practices before profits.

Amidst the impressive world headquarters of such famous names as Ragú Foods Co., Richardson-Vicks, Tetley Inc., and Forschner Group (U.S. distributor of the Swiss Army knife), there are quaint city streets where residents can still pop in a sweetshop for an ice cream sundae or stop and chat to a neighbor or business acquaintance. People get a lot of work done in Naugatuck Valley, but they still take time out for friendly hellos.

Surrounded on three sides by gently rolling hills, the Valley is a place where businesses and industries thrive, largely due to the hard work and Yankee ingenuity of its residents. The six communities that make up Naugatuck Valley (Ansonia, Derby, Oxford, Beacon Falls, Seymour, and Shelton) were first settled by European immigrants almost 350 years ago, boasting of a history that is only surpassed by its current endeavors.

Harnessing the power of the Housatonic and Naugatuck rivers, the Valley earned its reputation as an industry-rich area—"company towns" where the economy pivoted around several copper, brass, and rubber factories, heavy-machinery manufacturers, and metalworking plants. The smokestacks that jutted up into the sky stood as guardians over the Valley's economy.

As the times changed, so did the Naugatuck Valley. With the emergence of plastic substitutes and cheaper metal imports, Valley companies found old ways of operation sluggish and either closed or downsized businesses. Residents tackled the hard times with a steely determination, firing up their fierce pride and capitalizing on their well-developed transportation system and choice location. New businesses and industries arrived, at first mainly smaller precision manufacturing facilities, and later, high-technology companies. Industrial parks began to spring up and, in recent times, more than 100 new companies located in the area, migrating primarily from New York City and Fairfield County.

What the men and women who work for these companies are discovering—and what Valley residents have known all along—is that the Valley is a place with strong ties to both the past and the future, and that to people who live and work there, the Naugatuck Valley is more than an address. It is a way of life.

LOWER NAUGATUCK VALLEY CHAMBER OF COMMERCE

Geographic proximity does not always make for great neighbors, but in the case of the Lower Naugatuck Valley, a unified business climate has been fostered to the benefit of all with the help of the Lower Naugatuck Valley Chamber of Commerce.

Created in 1964 by a group of forward-looking business and professional people, the Lower Naugatuck Valley Chamber of Commerce has been a truly regional organization, covering the towns of Ansonia, Beacon Falls, Derby, Oxford, Seymour, and Shelton.

Its attempts to "break down the walls between the towns" have taken many avenues. The chamber was instrumental in forming the Valley Regional Planning Agency, which plans for transportation,

Phillips Medical Systems is one of the area's largest employers.

Griffin Hospital has faithfully served the Naugatuck Valley area since its doors opened in 1909.

Ansonia is one of the communities that is served by the Lower Naugatuck Valley Chamber of Commerce.

housing, and other concerns in the six-town region. The Valley Health District, which oversees public health affairs, was also organized through the chamber.

A strong commitment to community has also been fostered in its member towns through the chamber, which organized the local United Way in the mid-1960s. Its Junior Achievement program has also helped thousands of Valley youngsters get an inside look at business.

The chamber was instrumental in the formation of the Council of Governments, consisting of the Valley's municipal chief executives. The chamber also works closely with the Valley's five school superintendents, providing a conduit between education and the business community.

Information gathering

and sharing is an important goal of the chamber, which sponsors frequent luncheon sessions, where a forum is provided for discussing issues that affect local business and industry and where politicians and professionals share their expertise and philosophies.

All this has contributed to a new Valley—one that has outgrown its former image as an industrial mill town and now manages to attract corporate giants. The chamber has done much to develop a powerful community image, with projects aimed at spotlighting the Valley's strengths and its progress. Under the supervision of the Civic Brochure Committee, the Valley chamber produced a 48-page brochure that is being distributed to towns within a 20-minute commuting distance of the Valley, to show people that the Valley "is a great place to be," says Romolo D. Tedeschi, head of the Lower Naugatuck Valley Chamber of Commerce.

"We, indeed, have it all," he says, "from international headquarters to mom-and-pop shops that have been in business for generations." The brochure gives information about the history and economy of the Valley as well as its educational, housing, recreational, and other opportunities, and it touts the slogan, "We have it all in the Valley."

Route 8 carries visitors and residents through Naugatuck Valley.

W.E. BASSETT COMPANY

A high-fashion model in New York receives a manicure before she models priceless jewelry. A housewife in Illinois uses a fingernail clipper to work magic on dishpan hands.

As the world files and cuts, the W.E. Bassett Company has a hand in it all, producing an ever-growing line of quality manicure implements marketed under the Trim trademark. From a few thousand clippers per day in 1947, the demand for Trim products has steadily led to the production of many million a year, marketed to thousands of diversified retail outlets nationwide as well as to foreign markets and to armed forces worldwide.

The products are the mainstay of the W.E. Bassett Company, a leader among small industries in Naugatuck Valley. From its humble beginnings in 1939 as a contract machine shop, through the years of World War II (when the focus was on subcontract

The W.E. Bassett Company's Derby (ABOVE) and Shelton (LEFT) plants, where Trim manicure implements are manufactured and marketed.

manufacturing of military parts) to the present day, the firm has exhibited a desire for the continuous quality and improvement of its products.

Its entry into the manicure implement area was in 1947, with a fingernail clipper that was completely new in concept and design—one that placed emphasis on style and quality and made its mark in a highly competitive field.

The company was to grow

rapidly with founder William Bassett devoting his energies to management, new product development, and advertising. His brother Harry Bassett was in charge of production. Harry, who came aboard in 1943, served for many years as president and chief executive officer. He is currently chairman of the board.

The firm is now managed by the founder's two sons: William C. Bassett, who joined the company in

1963, is now president and treasurer; and David Bassett, who came aboard in 1968, is now secretary.

The company moved into a new plant in Derby in 1952. Many new items were added, and the plant expanded five times. In 1978 a second plant was built in Shelton, serving as the company's headquarters.

This homegrown Naugatuck Valley company has provided uninterrupted employment for a sizable number of Valley residents, and it contributes to many civic and charitable community activities. According to Harry Bassett, it owes much of its success to its loyal group of long-term employees. Working as a team, the individuals who comprise the W.E. Bassett Company never lose sight of their goal to produce the finest products of their kind in the world.

GRIFFIN HOSPITAL

A young woman looks with incredible joy at her newborn baby. The birthing experience has been made extra special for her and her family at Griffin Hospital's Childbirth Center, which has set the standard for obstetric care in Connecticut. The Childbirth Center is an example of Griffin Hospital's slogan: "Good Medicine for Our Community."

A man who had trouble breathing and who could not climb a flight of stairs without stopping every few steps to rest learned how to breath better and feel better at Griffin Hospital's Pulmonary Rehabilitation Program. And an elderly woman, told by her physician that she needs to lose weight or face serious health complications, is determined to get lean and eat healthy food. Each week she heads to the Griffin Hospital cafeteria to stock up on Healthy Helpings, nutritious and delicious frozen dinners

The Southford Medical Center, offering coordinated health care under one roof, extends Griffin's reach into the community.

for people on restricted diets. These instances are also examples of "Good Medicine for Our Community."

Griffin Hospital's slogan is not only about prescription drugs and treatments or about surgery and procedures. It is about an attitude of commitment and innovation—about the hospital's vision for the people of the community to live the happiest, healthiest lives possible. Founded in 1909, the hospital, now part of Griffin Health Services Corporation, has evolved with the community and kept pace with its needs.

including a rocking chair, a cradle, and a sleeper lounge chair for overnight guests.

There is a Jacuzzi available for moms-to-be to help provide natural pain relief. New parents are also treated to a gourmet celebration dinner with special touches such as champagne, birthday cake, and flowers.

From birth and beyond, Griffin Hospital delivers a lifetime of services. It is the only hospital in the state to offer its own health maintenance organization. Introduced in 1986, the Suburban Health Plan helps area businesses better manage their health benefit dollars while ensuring quality services for their employees.

The Southford Medical Center in Southbury and the Family Health Center in Shelton extend Griffin Hospital's reach into the community, housing primary care physicians and specialists who provide convenient, coordinated health care under one roof.

Griffin's central outpatient and short-term surgery programs make it easy for patients to utilize such ser-

ABOVE: Griffin's Convenient Care Service, backed by the full resources of the emergency room, offers exceptional care for those in need of a doctor.

LEFT: A wide variety of treatment and services assure that Griffin Hospital provides "Good Medicine for Our Community."

A shining example of this is its Childbirth Center, equipped to provide women and their families with a full range of childbirth options in a modern, homelike atmosphere that fosters family unity while maintaining physical safety. Private postpartum rooms have oak furniture,

vices as mammography, osteoporosis screenings, and same-day surgical procedures, such as cataract removal. Its cardiology department provides diagnostic testing, a pacemaker clinic, and a cardiac rehabilitation center.

Convenient Care is a special service of the hospital's emergency department that specializes in minor emergencies, such as cuts, bruises, flu, colds, sore throats, and poison ivy and is backed by the full resources of Griffin's medical staff and hospital.

The hospital also offers Optifast®, a medically supervised weight-reduction program for people 50 pounds or 30 percent over their ideal weight. The program is at medical sites in Seymour, Southbury, Shelton, and Fairfield.

A variety of other innovative programs are available through Griffin Health Services. Medsource refers patients to more than 100 physicians. Mature Advantage provides specialized programs for people ages 55 and older, such as discounts on prescriptions, vision care, dental care, hearing aids, and examinations as well as free educational programs, assistance with billing and insurance forms, and special activities and travel packages.

Griffin Home Care arranges for services at home or help to obtain needed medical equipment. The Chores and More program helps provide domestic, yard, shopping, and errand services, and Wellness Works provides such services as nutrition counseling, cholesterol screening, and fitness testing for individuals, groups, and businesses.

Behind every innovative pro-

gram are health care professionals from a variety of backgrounds who dedicate their lives to caring for the members of their community.

Griffin Hospital sports a long and proud tradition. Named for George Griffing, a Shelton button maker who donated to the hospital securities worth more than $65,000, the hospital was opened on December 6, 1909, as a 24-bed structure, erected at a total cost of $40,495.

Griffin Hospital and its parent company serve as a reflection of the community—growing and changing to meet the health and life-style needs of the community. Working to ensure a better today and an ever brighter tomorrow by providing "Good Medicine for Our Community."

LEFT: Griffin's hotel-like Patient Room Service staff adds to the comfort of one's stay.

BELOW: Griffin Hospital has set the standards for obstetric and pediatric care in Connecticut.

GREAT COUNTRY BANK

In 1862 Ansonia residents discovered the path to financial security up one flight of stairs of a modest brick building at 167 Main Street. It was there that the Savings Bank of Ansonia, later to become Great Country Bank, was founded by a group of community-minded individuals who believed Ansonia needed a place where savings could be protected and earn interest. They also saw the bank as an institution that could become a leader in helping the town achieve its full potential.

In 1900, one year after the borough of Ansonia became a town, a new home for the bank was built at 117 Main Street—an attractive, new building outfitted with what was then state-of-the-art equipment. By 1915 the bank's substantial growth as the community's savings center made it one of the state's leading banking institutions. During the period from 1922 to 1954 the bank experienced tremendous growth. Dividends increased by 288 percent during this time, while surplus funds skyrocketed by 1,152 percent.

Things kept getting bigger and better, and on October 30, 1961, more than 6,000 members of the community celebrated the opening

Great Country's main office in Ansonia.

of the bank's new offices at 211 Main Street. To commemorate the open house as well as the bank's upcoming century anniversary, every depositor was offered a special anniversary dividend of an additional one-quarter percent interest. The bank's new home proved to be a significant part of the city's redevelopment program as well as a demonstration of the depth of its commitment to the community.

In 1964 the bank passed the $50-million mark in assets; less than eight years later, in 1972, it doubled that figure. Another major achievement of the 1970s involved conversion from a manual to computer operation.

Soon afterward the bank began expanding, with new branch offices opening in Seymour in 1970, Shelton in 1972, and Beacon Falls in 1973. To support the growth brought in by these branches, a new wing and a second story were added to the main office in 1977. These additions gave the bank the ways and means to support its commitment to serve a diverse and growing customer base in the increasingly competitive climate of deregulation that was to follow.

In 1985 a new name was chosen for the bank to symbolize its great pride in the people of the Valley and

This building at 117 Main Street was home to the Great Country Bank between 1900 and 1961.

the American way of life. On November 12 the Savings Bank of Ansonia officially became Great Country Bank. Another important milestone occurred in 1986 with the conversion of Great Country Bank from a mutual savings bank to a capital stock savings bank. This changeover further enhanced its strong capital base, providing the bank with an even greater opportunity for growth and to expand its range of financial services.

In recent times much attention and effort has been given to the renovation and expansion of branch offices. A second office was opened in Shelton; a larger and more modern facility was built at Coram Avenue; the old Terry Building at 200 Main Street was renovated to bring departments housed in the Shelton facility closer to the main office for increased operational efficiency, and the Hamden loan office was expanded into a highly successful full-service branch operation. At this office the concept of One-to-One banking was introduced. Through this unique approach to one-stop banking, tellers are specially trained on state-of-the-art computer terminals to work individually with customers on everything from balance inquiries to loan amortization schedules.

Classic 50 members receive discount coupons quarterly for preferred savings through area merchants.

Great Country Investment Services provides brokerage services offered through Mabon, Nugent & Company, Members New York Stock Exchange Inc., and other principal exchanges, SIPC. Customers receive expert advice on personal financial planning, a wide variety of quality investment products, and the convenience of investing right where they bank.

Over the past 128 years Great Country Bank has continually earned the trust and confidence of its customers through its selection of qual-

LEFT: The Terry Building at 200 Main Street is home to the bank's consumer loan, mortgage, and other administrative offices.

BELOW: Recently, a second Great Country Bank branch was opened on Coram Avenue in Shelton.

The bank also prides itself on offering the best checking packages in the area. All of Great Country's personal checking accounts include "Buyers Advantage," 90-day purchase replacement, and extended warranty protection on purchases paid for in full with a Great Country Bank check. Through the Club Checking Program customers choose the type of checking account that best suits their needs. Club I offers free checking plus interest with a minimum balance of $100, $100,000 accidental death insurance, and a free first order of personalized checks. Club II requires no minimum balance and includes interest on checking, an additional $10,000 accidental death insurance, free personalized checks, free travelers checks, return or non-return checking, and instant overdraft protection—all for only five dollars a month. Both programs also include 16 additional benefits at no charge.

Classic 50, a checking package

for customers age 50 and over, was recently introduced to meet the special financial needs of this segment of the community. Like Club Checking, Classic 50 offers many additional benefits at no extra charge, including a local merchant discount program. Through this unique program

ity financial products, a commitment to excellence in customer service, and a deep sense of responsibility to the community. These qualities that have distinguished the bank in the past will continue to do so into the next century as they are clearly the essence of great banking.

CURTISS-RYAN, INC.

When someone walks into Curtiss-Ryan, Inc., and hands over a check for a new Honda, they get more than they bargained for—in the best sense of the phrase. They get "more" as in more for their money, better service, and a well-stocked parts department with more than $300,000 in genuine Honda parts.

At Curtiss-Ryan the philosophy is that purchasing an automobile is not a simple exchange of car for cash. It should be a working partnership between the customer and the

Curtiss-Ryan Honda is "The house that service built." Partners George J. Ryan and Richard Foehrenbach have strived since 1971 to make excellent service and fair prices their top priorities.

dealership. And a low price makes a great first impression.

But if a low price is all customers get, Curtiss-Ryan partners George J. Ryan and Richard Foehrenbach believe automobile consumers are short-changing themselves. Price, efficient service, and professional care should be a package deal. A customer not only needs the best deal but the best dealership, because today's customers keep their cars longer than five years.

Since 1971 Ryan and Foehrenbach have been committed to making service and fair price the dealership's top priorities. They have become known throughout the Valley and Connecticut as "The house that service built," and their efforts

have been rewarded by the fact that six out of every 10 people who buy a car from Curtiss-Ryan come back for a second purchase.

The dealership has also won numerous awards throughout the years for for adhering to the highest industry standards. Most recently, Ryan was given the 1989 Outstanding Dealer Award by *Time* magazine for his outstanding performance as a dealer and for his contributions to the community.

Such an emphasis on superior performance is prevalent through the dealership, with the entire staff striving to provide customers the right car and the right options for their particular needs. Curtiss-Ryan salespeople have done their homework, constantly studying the latest advances in the automobile field. They know what they're talking about.

Each salesperson is also committed to taking the hassle out of purchasing a new or used vehicle, helping with anything from car registration to insurance transfers to financing plans.

Above all, the staff of Curtiss-Ryan will go the extra mile to be considerate and give customers the courtesy they deserve. And behind every salesperson are efficient support personnel and office staff (who know the importance of keeping track of critical paperwork) as well as exceptional service technicians—people who all work together to ensure that at Curtiss-Ryan, Inc., service makes the difference.

BRENNAN CONSTRUCTION COMPANY

Brennan Construction, located at 223 Canal Street in Shelton, goes forward into the twenty-first century with the same enthusiasm and dedication to the construction industry that has ensured its success since its founding in 1897.

The family business, nearly 100 years in existence and celebrating 93 years in Shelton in 1990, started as a masonry and concrete placement contractor. By the mid-1930s the firm diversified into general construction, serving the industrial construction needs of such Valley industrial plants as B.F. Goodrich, Anaconda American Brass, Uniroyal, and Farrel Corporation. Brennan Construction remained predominantly an industrial contractor until the mid-1960s, when the changing face of the Valley pushed the company into pursuing other fields. Banks, health care facilities, senior citizen housing, corporate offices, education and law enforcement institutions, as well as retail and environmental control buildings became the new endeavors. Derby Savings Bank main branch office in Derby and branch office in Shelton, ITT Semi Conductor, Griffin Hospital Emergency Room, Pitney Bowes, the Oxford Town Hall, Derby Superior Courthouse, the

Brennan Construction Company was located on Cliff Street in Shelton. Photo circa 1900

The Derby Savings Bank main branch on Main Street in downtown Derby was constructed by Brennan and completed in the 1970s.

Shelton Police Headquarters, Lafayette School, Hewitt Memorial Hospital, and the Plumb Memorial Library Expansion in Shelton are only some of the projects undertaken throughout the Valley.

By no means is the company confined to the Valley. "Our skills and services are evident statewide," states vice president Thomas Brennan. The distinguished list of clients includes General Electric World Headquarters in Fairfield; Boehringer Ingelheim in Ridgefield; Yale and Fairfield universities; Bridgeport, Yale New Haven, and Milford hospitals; as well as American Cyanamid, Nestle Foods, and Showcase Cinemas/National Amusements. Many of these firms and others have awarded Brennan Construction multiple contracts of varying size over the years.

The strengths of the Brennan Company are the efforts of talented, conscientious, dedicated employees of the family-owned firm. "The Brennans are actively involved as managers. While each one has separate duties, our responsibilities overlap in that we all take a personal interest in each and every project. At any given time, there is a Brennan pre-

sent on the job," says Robert J. Brennan, president.

Recently the firm has again diversified and expanded business to include highway and bridge work statewide. In addition to the actual constuction, Brennan is very mindful of job safety and the environment. Modern, well-maintained equipment, combined with safety training, seminars, and courses, ensures job safety. Pollution and soil erosion controls are utilized to protect the environment. The company has been commended on the care taken to protect the wetlands on one recent project as well as the effort made to divert a river through bypass piping to protect fish swimming upstream to spawn.

Brennan Construction Company employees are proud of who they are and what they do, and they are proud to be based in a progressive community like Shelton. Brennan looks with confidence to the next decade and the beginning of its second 100 years in business, meeting tomorrow's needs.

DERBY SAVINGS BANK

It all began with three dollars and a shoe store. In August 1846 the Derby Society for Savings, which changed its name 10 years later to the Derby Savings Bank, opened for business in what was known as Sidney Downs' shoe store on the south side of Main Street and received its first deposit of three dollars.

For the men who were counted among its incorporators, who included many civic and community leaders, it was a vision realized—a culmination of an idea that had been first explored by the group in a meeting called by Edward Shelton and held in the basement of St. James Church in Derby.

As a result of their efforts, the bank was incorporated by the Connecticut General Assembly in June 1846, the same year Iowa became a state, the sewing machine was patented by Elias Howe, the Smithsonian Institution was founded, and John Galle discovered the planet Neptune.

The first officers of the bank were John Howe, president; Edward Shelton, vice president; and Joseph Canfield, secretary and treasurer. Fitch Smith, David Bassett, George Blakeman, Thomas Wallace, Sr., Samuel French, Henry Hubbard, and Sheldon Smith, Jr., were elected as directors.

The bank's first loan was made on September 22, 1846, amounting to $600. The bank's first dividend was declared on January 1, 1847, for

The old bank building at the corner of Main and Caroline streets was occupied by Derby Savings Bank between the years 1859 and 1923.

$11.43 at the rate of 5 percent.

In 1857 the bank was moved to the second story of a building on the northwest corner of Caroline and Main streets, which was built by the Birmingham National Bank (formerly the Manufacturers' Bank). It continued to transact business there until 1893, when the greater portion of the building was torn down and rebuilt. In a "Souvenir History" of Derby and Shelton issued by the *Evening Transcript* in 1896, it was noted that the

building "contains a vault protected by every known device and undoubtedly affords a security as ample and complete as human skill has yet devised." The building is now the home of the Polish Eagle Hall.

In 1923 Derby Savings Bank moved to 315 Main Street at the corner of Main and Olivia, which served as its headquarters for more than a half-century. The building today serves as the law offices of Cohen, Micci, Thomas, and Stamos.

In 1976 Derby Savings Bank moved to what is now the site of its main office at One Elizabeth Street. The bank's corporate headquarters

are now located at 33 Elizabeth Street.

In 1976, after the state legislature passed a law allowing for the first time in history for savings banks to offer checking accounts, Derby Savings Bank became one of the first savings banks in the state to do so as well as to offer automatic teller machine services. This ushered in a new era for the bank providing a foundation for solid growth and expansion.

Today the bank has spread throughout Naugatuck Valley and elsewhere. Presently there are branch locations in Derby at the Orange/Derby shopping center in Shelton on Howe Avenue and at the Huntington Village Shopping Center, in Seymour on New Haven Road, in Orange on

In 1923 the bank built a new home at the corner of Main and Olivia streets, and this building served as its headquarters for more than 50 years.

Old Tavern Road, in Southbury on Main Street, in Trumbull on White Plains Road, in Stratford on Main Street, and in Avon on Meadow Lane. In addition, there are two loan production offices, which operate independently at the Orange and Southbury locations.

As of May 15, 1990, bank deposits totaled $460 million, with $610 million in total assets and $543 million out in loans.

The mission of Derby Savings Bank is to operate as a state chartered, flexible, profitable stock institution providing market-driven

financial services. Through the years, the bank has exhibited a strong commitment to the communities in which it serves. Its contribution to the area, both financial and otherwise, have been widespread and wide ranging. Perhaps it was most accurately summed up in the 1896 "Souvenir History" of the *Evening Transcript,* wherein is contained the following: "Very few realize what a potent agency this old, conservative, and prosperous institution has been in building up this and the surrounding places, or what it has done to encourage thriftiness in the wage earner and to teach people habits of savings, industry, and virtues that underlie good citizenship."

HERSHEY METAL PRODUCTS, INC.

The Hershey plant in Ansonia does not make chocolate bars, but in its seven decades of operation, it has made just about everything else.

A versatile company, Hershey Metal Products, Inc., has proven to be a master with metal, in tune with the times producing items to meet the needs and wants of the public, the government, and the business world. Its products have ranged from configurations included on the LEM (lunar excursion module) that ferried astronauts to the moon to a popular tap used in bars and restaurants for beer kegs.

The company was first housed in a small facility on Hawkins Street in Derby, and later, in an additional facility on Division Street in Ansonia, where both operations were consolidated in the late 1970s. In 1987 the company developed the Hershey Industrial Park, where its entire operation is now located.

It all started with the ingenuity of one man, toolmaker Paul Hershey, who, in 1920, purchased the tools and assets of a small garage shop that had been closed after World War I. He moved the business to Hawkins Street and began to manufacture a variety of products and components ranging from radio condensers to pen and pencil sets for desks.

Collectors of animal figures may have some of Hershey's Liggett Kennel Club products in their menagerie, miniature cast likenesses of dogs, which in the 1940s sold for 45 cents for the small version and 85 cents for the larger.

In the 1930s the company continued to produce a variety of products—ashtrays, cigarette holders, and lighters. The firm even added a division called Derby Sealers, which made and marketed tape-dispensing machines—a division that was eventually sold to 3M in the mid-1960s.

In the late 1930s Hershey Metal Products started making mili-

Toolmaker Paul Hershey began Hershey Metal Products, Inc., in 1920.

tary hardware both for the United States and the Allies. The booming war economy translated into peak times for the Valley firm, and in 1942 it bought its Division Street facility. Both plants geared up to manufacture 50-caliber machine gun projectiles.

"We made over 2 million projectiles per month," recalls John

Frey, the company's current president. "It was the high point of our company in terms of employment. At the time we had more than 600 workers in the two plants."

After the war the company again adapted to a peacetime economy, making a variety of different products, including lubricating equipment and replacement parts for auto suspension systems.

However America was at battle again all too soon, and during the Korean War Hershey was once more in production making projectiles. "We decided in the mid-1950s that we would not be dependent on that kind of military work. We took thoughtfully calculated steps to determine our future," says Frey.

The first move was to start a subsidiary called Penn Keystone, which fabricated instruments for military aircraft at its Hawkins Street plant, which was sold some two decades later. The equipment was "the simplest, safest way to report general information," such as the position of landing gear. One of the subsidiary's

One of the company's major products is the Hoff-Stevens tap, a draft-beer tapping device for kegs.

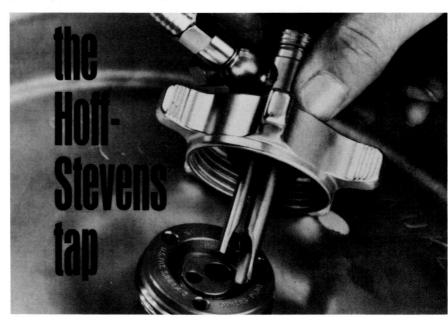

products was the Peaklite indicators, a special light contained on Xerox and other copying machines that told when the machine was ready to copy. It was during this time when the company made a special "bank of lights" to be used on the LEM, which was used to indicate when the long legs of the module touch the solid surface of the moon.

In the mid-1960s the company came up with one of its most popular products to date, which is still in production. More than a half-million beer kegs have been connected to the special beer tapping device. The special tap provided the bulk of business in the 1960s and 1970s, along with contract hardware. In the 1980s the demand for beer taps started to recede, and Hershey Metal Products, Inc., was reorganized to focus on the production of hardware assemblies

During the flood of 1955 Hershey's Division Street plant was flooded with more than eight feet of water.

such as tap wrenches and circle cutters—more than 100 different items in all that are marketed for the home hobby shop and tool rooms.

In the twenty-first century this flexible firm might be making anything. "We will try just about anything we think our equipment can make and our people can operate. When we worked on the LEM, we really had no idea what we were getting into," says Frey. "Fortunately it worked out great, and I think it was more than luck. In my experience good luck is a by-product of hard work and good old-fashioned Yankee ingenuity."

Special configurations developed by Hershey were used on NASA's LEM (lunar excursion module), which landed on the moon.

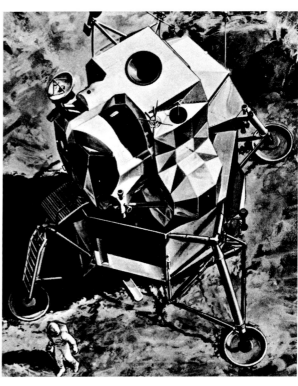

SUMMAGRAPHICS CORPORATION

At the world renowned Johns Hopkins Medical Institution, Dr. Alan Partin uses a Summagraphics® digitizer to study how cancer cells move and change. From a college dormitory room at Duke University, a student named Seth Watkins collaborates with NASA to grow purer silicone crystals in space, using a Summagraphics digitizer.

Digitizers produced by this Seymour, Connecticut, company are the key to computer-aided design, manufacturing, engineering (CAD/CAM/CAE), and other industries. Digitizers are used to input graphics, handwriting, and batched software commands into a form that can be easily manipulated on a computer screen. The digitizers consist of a tablet and a hand-held pointer (either cursor or stylus) that translate graphic data and mathematical coordinates into digital language that

computers understand.

The applications are virtually limitless, encompassing fields as diverse as art restoration, aviation, weather forecasting, and printing. Using a digitizer and the proper software, a person can do anything from designing an automobile or creating three-dimensional landscape elevations to analyzing handwriting or helping to create animated images.

In May 1990 Summagraphics acquired Houston Instrument, including its manufacturing plant in Belgium. Houston Instrument, a computer peripherals manufacturer, was founded in 1969 in Houston, Texas. Presently headquartered in Austin, Texas, it manufactures and markets pen plotters, cutters, and large-format scanners used in computer-aided design systems.

Summagraphics believes that the two companies will complement each other well—their combined

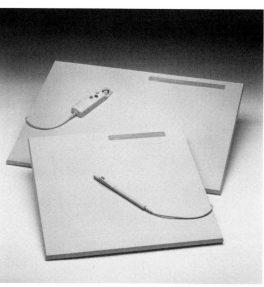

Summagraphics Digitizers consist of a tablet and a hand-held cursor or stylus pointer that translates graphic data and mathematical coordinates into digital language that computers understand.

products result in a broad range of computer graphic peripherals that are key suppliers to the PC/CAD market. The Summagraphics acquisition program is focused on businesses that are compatible and synergistic with its own.

Summagraphics Corporation is recognized as a world leader in the design, manufacture, and marketing of computer-graphic peripheral products, selling products to original equipment manufacturers (OEMs)

for integration into manufacturer-configured systems, as well as to users directly through an extensive network of domestic and international distributors.

From the company's best-selling SummaSketch® product line to large, highly precise Microgrid® tablets for sophisticated users, Summagraphics' products are recognized as industry standards and price/performance leaders.

Summagraphics' continued success can be attributed to a variety of reasons: technological leadership, competitive pricing, and experienced and enthusiastic management. The underlying factor, however, is the firm's dedication to manufacturing technologically advanced products of high quality and to maintaining high standards of service.

Summagraphics Corporation technology has opened up new worlds for thousands of people with numerous applications, becoming an extension of the user's creativity and proving to be as limitless as the imagination.

Houston Instrument manufactures and markets large-format plotters used in computer-aided design systems. The DMP™–61 DL and the DMP–62 DL are both equipped to handle oversized material.

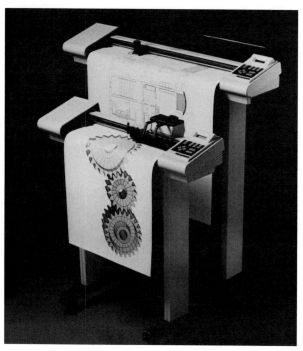

PETROL PLUS

When the company that was to become Petrol Plus was founded in the early twentieth century, the few automobiles on the road were called horseless carriages, and the phrase "two-car family" had yet to be coined.

Today thousands of motorists each day throughout the Valley and the rest of the state "fill 'er up" at Petrol Plus or other household name stations that obtain their petroleum products from the Derby-based firm.

Petrol Plus, which has become one of the largest independent companies of its kind in the region, also distributes a number of other petroleum products, such as lubricating oils for industry, fuel oil products, and motor oils. The firm also operates a number of convenience stores in Connecticut under a variety of names.

It all began some 85 years ago, when Arthur Goldstein started making and distributing charcoal. In the 1930s he purchased the Bristol Coal Company, located at the company's present base of operations on Commerce Street, renaming the firm the Derby Coal and Charcoal Company.

Petrol Plus' newest Snaxx Plus® convenience store and gasoline station, located in Oxford, Connecticut.

He also built an inland terminal on the property, no longer in use, but once a busy port where barges traveling the Housatonic River would offload their oil into the company's large tanks.

When Goldstein died in 1939, his wife, Edith, headed the company until 1945, when her son Robert Goldstein and son-in-law Gerald Bogen took over the reins. Gerald's wife, Helen, was also active in the day-to-day operations of the firm.

From 1945 until 1971 the firm experienced rapid growth, branching out into air conditioning installations, specializing in large commercial as well as residential jobs. During that period the company became one of the largest distributors of home heating oils, and in the mid-1950s its name was changed to the Derby Oil Company.

In 1971 the firm was sold to

Arthur Bogen (left), executive vice president, and Arthur Goldstein, president.

Mobil Oil Corporation, and Goldstein and Bogen formed Petrol Plus, shifting their focus to the distribution of gasoline. In 1974 Goldstein's son Arthur, who is currently president, came aboard, followed the next year by Bogen's son Arthur, who is now executive vice president. The senior Bogen serves as chairman of the board. Ken Koufman is the firm's director of wholesale marketing.

The family atmosphere pervades the entire firm, with a number of longtime staffers who are just like family, and who, like the direct descendants of Petrol Plus' past presidents and officers, are dedicated to providing the upmost in service and quality.

VALLEY CABLE VISION, INC.

A pioneering spirit, a commitment to community and customer, and a sense of family have been the hallmarks of Valley Cable Vision since its inception in 1965. That year founder George I. Reynolds applied for the cable franchise for the area of Ansonia, Beacon Falls, Bethany, Derby, Naugatuck, Oxford, Seymour, and Shelton. The franchise was awarded in 1967, but legal delays prevented the system from going into operation until 1972, when the first subscribers were connected, making Valley Cable the second active cable system in the state of Connecticut.

By 1990 Valley Cable had in excess of 40,000 subscribers representing 80 percent of the homes in the franchise area. This percentage is well above the national average of 55 percent.

Valley Cable Vision has been headed by Jeffrey Reynolds, George's son. Four other sons, James, Robert, Fred, and David, have all been involved in the family's other cable operations in the state of New York.

The company's more than 100 employees are a part of the Valley Cable family. They work within a system of participative management that encourages innovation, growth, and teamwork. This same philosophy has been extended to the customers, who are at the heart of the business.

Since its beginning, Valley Cable Vision has been regarded as a pioneer in the industry. This reputation can be attributed in part to the company's commitment to state-of-the-art technology.

Valley Cable is the only dual cable system in the state, giving it twice the channel capacity of single cable systems. One of the first companies in the country to purchase an earth station when satellite technol-

ogy became available in the mid-1970s, Valley Cable was also among the nation's first cable systems to offer such services as Home Box Office (HBO), Cable News Network (CNN), and ESPN. These early offerings reflected an entrepreneurial stance toward programming, which differentiated Valley Cable from more conservative systems.

In 1983 Valley Cable was again in the forefront as one of the first in the country to utilize "addressable" converters, now a standard in the industry. Through addressability special computer-controlled converters provide expanded viewing and service. In addition, this technology affords the option for pay-per-view programming, which allows special events to be ordered on an individual basis.

Another area in which Valley Cable has been in the vanguard is advertising. Specialized equipment enables the company to insert commercials on certain national cable networks, providing local merchants the opportunity for greater and easier access to a wider advertising market.

Since its inception Valley Cable has been located on Great Hill Road

Members of the Reynolds family: (from left) George Reynolds, Jeffrey Reynolds, Frederick Reynolds, and James Reynolds.

in Seymour. More than just a cable operation, the modern, 32,000-square-foot building is a complete media center also housing the facilities of Sound Concepts, a sister company, which produces corporate videos along with radio and television commercials. Through the years the firm has won numerous awards, including several CLIOs, the broadcast industry's international award for advertising.

Bridgeways Communication's Channel 43 has also operated out of the facility, as does the Connecticut

The company's more than 100 employees work within a system of participative management that encourages innovation, growth, and teamwork.

Valley Cable studios have been the scene of special programs, such as gubernatorial and senatorial debates as well as shows concerning current events, the law, and health care.

Cable Network, a division of Valley Cable that sells regional advertising time for other cable systems throughout the state. Transmitters for the public broadcast station WMNR, C-Med, and the Community College Network have all been located at Valley Cable on company-donated tower space.

In addition to being in the forefront of technology, Valley Cable Vision has been a recognized leader in local programming. Valley Cable's studios have been the scene of special programs, such as gubernatorial and senatorial debates, as well as other shows featuring local, state, and national officials. As the founder of the Connecticut Cable Interconnect, Valley Cable has distributed these live programs to more than 500,000 homes throughout the state.

Coverage of high school football, local elections, public hearings as well as shows concerning current events, the law, and health care

have been standard fare on Channel 10B, Valley Cable's local community channel.

Valley Cable Vision programming has been nominated for the prestigious ACE award, the cable television equivalent of the Oscar, a total of eight times. Competing nationally against cable operators many times its size, Valley Cable has brought home three ACE awards.

Another distinguishing quality of Valley Cable has been its commitment to community service. The company has done numerous projects, including telethons for Toys for Tots and for the Valley Association of Retarded Children and Adults. Each year the company has produced a special video for the United Way campaign.

In addition to these special projects, the company contributes to the community on a regular basis in both dollars and services. Many Valley Cable employees have also

been active in a wide range of community organizations.

While the company has received numerous awards for its contributions, nowhere is Valley Cable's commitment to the community and its pioneer spirit in the industry better exemplified than by the efforts of George and Jeffrey Reynolds. Both are considered leaders in cable television, as evidenced by their joint receipt of the Connecticut Cable Television Association's Pioneer Award for commitment to excellence. Jeffrey also was given the National Cable Television Association's President's Award for continuing service to the industry.

An acknowledged community leader as well, Jeffrey received both the Valley Chamber of Commerce's Gold Seal Award and the Valley United Way's Charles Flynn Humanitarian Award for outstanding service to the local community.

A spirit of innovation, quality service, and family is the tradition of Valley Cable Vision—a tradition that extends to staff, customers, and community.

Valley Cable Vision was one of the first companies in the country to purchase an earth station when satellite technology became available in the mid-1970s.

TETLEY INC.

Throughout the hamlets and farmlands of the Yorkshire moors, brothers Edward and Joseph Tetley rode like the wind, selling tea from the back of their pack horses. Against this picturesque background, Tetley Inc. got its start in 1837, beginning a tradition of innovation and quality that has lasted more than a century and a half.

In 1856 Joseph took over the business, moving the company to London and subsequently introducing Tetley tea to the United States. An innovative marketer, Joseph merchandised his tea in department stores, a move considered a radical marketing approach at the time. He took an important step in the history of the firm in 1913, establishing plants in New York City and Savannah, Georgia. At that time the product line was expanded to not only include loose tea but tea bags, first introduced by an enterprising merchant in little silk bags in 1910.

A third plant was opened in 1958 on the banks of the Susquehanna River in Williamsport, Pennsylvania, which, along with the

Canny marketing and merchandising has been an important part of the Tetley tradition.

Savannah plant, continues to manufacture tea bags today.

The "tiny little tea leaves" in Tetley tea come from various tea-growing countries around the world and are truly tiny because Tetley uses only new growth (which are the smaller leaves on the tea bush) because these make the finest quality teas. One bag might contain 25 to 30

different teas to guarantee both the uniformity and the taste customers have come to expect from Tetley tea.

Tea has taken many forms since Joseph Tetley sold loose tea from horseback. As a monument to his innovation Tetley has continued to expand its product line to satisfy the tastes of modern consumers. In addition to loose tea and individual tea bags, the company makes family and half-gallon size tea bags, one-ounce food service iced tea bags, instant and iced tea mixes, iced tea crystals, decaffeinated tea, flavored tea mixes, as well as canned and bottled teas. Such products are sold to consumers through grocery and specialty stores and served by many fine hotels, restaurants, and other food-service outlets.

Tetley also provides a strong presence in the U.S. coffee market, offering a wide selection of premium coffees with well-known brand names such as Martinson, Savarin, Bustelo, Medaglia D'Oro, Brown Gold, El Pico, and Oquendo.

The coffee business shares the same tradition of innovation and quality that characterizes the tea business. Joe Martinson, founder of Martinson Coffee Company, possessed an entrepreneurial spirit much like that of Joseph Tetley. In 1898 he roasted and blended fresh coffee beans purchased at the New York Harbor and sold them to his lower east side neighbors from a pushcart. He started his first factory in 1908 and began selling his personal blend to city restaurants.

Martinson coffee has been famous for its quality since the turn of the century. To literally drive home the point to his customers that he was selling premium coffee, Martinson purchased a fleet of Rolls Royces, painted the company name on them, and used them as delivery vehicles.

The Bustelo Coffee Roasting Company specializes in espresso

Joe Martinson used a fleet of Rolls Royces as delivery vehicles to impress on his customers the premium quality of his coffee.

Martinson. Coffee used to be delivered in a Rolls-Royce.

coffees, Cafe Bustelo, and Cafe Oquendo. In 1928 Gregorio Bustelo developed the coffee that bears his name by blending selected beans and roasting them dark to achieve the coffee flavor he savored in his native country. He began by supplying a few Hispanic restaurants and groceries and expanded to the point where it is the number-one selling espresso in the United States. Bustelo's catchy slogan is well known in many Spanish communities: *"Digan, lo que digan . . . En mi casa toman Bustelo"* (translation: Say what you want to say . . . In my house we drink Bustelo.)

S.A. Schonbrunn Co., Inc., enhanced Tetley's coffee operations when it was acquired by the firm in 1982. Schonbrunn's leading brand, Savarin, the brand of El Exigente, was named after a famous French chef.

Premium coffee beans used in making Savarin today preserve its quality heritage. Schonbrunn also brought to Tetley two specialty coffees—Medaglia D'Oro and El Pico espressos. Medaglia D'Oro has been the favorite of coffee connoisseurs for generations, and El Pico is a staple in many Spanish-American households. Rounding out the Schonbrunn line is Brown Gold, a premium, 100 percent Colombian coffee known for its smooth, mild taste.

Tetley's commitment to inno-

ABOVE: Tetley Inc.'s Naugatuck Valley headquarters.

LEFT: Tea tasting in the classic tradition circa 1900.

vation and quality exemplified by Joseph Tetley, Joe Martinson, Sam Schonbrunn, Gregorio Bustelo, and others continues today. Market innovation, the production of a quality product, and personalized customer service are the cornerstones of the Tetley philosophy. This commitment to excellence on the part of employees assures success in the markets in which the company competes.

Tetley Inc. now ranks second nationally in the output of tea products, and the firm is a leader in several coffee market segments. While tea and coffee are the firm's mainstays, Tetley also produces a variety of other beverages and is continuing to develop additional items and to explore new markets.

RICHARDSON-VICKS

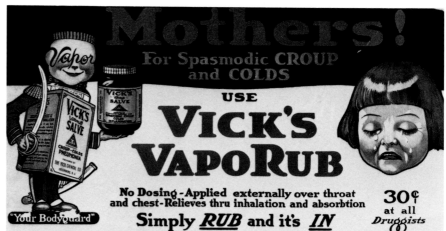

LEFT: Smith Richardson was an innovative marketing man. He pioneered the use of couponing and direct mail sampling in his efforts to keep the fledgling business growing.

ABOVE: The promise of an external treatment for children's colds and croup, delivered in outdoor and in–store advertising, helped convince mothers early in the century to try Vicks VapoRub.

The time was 1905; the place was Greensboro, North Carolina. When families started sniffling and sneezing, they turned for relief to Lunsford Richardson, a pharmacist who developed 21 home remedies under the name Vicks.

One of these products was to become legendary: a vaporizing salve for colds that used menthol from Japan. Rubbed on the chest, where it stimulated blood flow, it made the chest feel pleasingly warm; body heat vaporized the menthol in the salve and soothing and medicated vapors could be inhaled for hours.

When Richardson died in 1919, his Vicks VapoRub was a household word with national sales at about $3 million; this was substantial progress for a man who at age 51 sunk his life savings of $8,000 to start the Vick Family Remedies Company. Today that company is known as Richardson-Vicks, and it operates as part of the health and beauty care business of the Procter & Gamble Company.

Richardson-Vicks became part of the Valley community when it opened a research center in Shelton in 1982 and expanded its presence by adding marketing and sales operations on the 75-acre site in 1989. The

Shelton complex provides state-of-the art research facilities, manifesting the company's proven commitment to creating quality consumer products. The staff in Shelton is devoted to the development and marketing of new and better products to meet consumers' health care and beauty care needs.

Lunsford Richardson would have been proud to see the results his efforts have yielded but probably not surprised to learn of the many products the company went on to produce—everything from Oil of Olay beauty fluid to Fixodent denture adhesive to Vicks NyQuil nighttime cold medicine.

In the beginning such progress could hardly seem possible. The firm came perilously close to failing within the first two years, but it was rescued by Lunsford's son Smith, who, as sales manager, displayed abundant foresight and creativity. Today he would be called a turnaround expert, and 1990s marketers would find much to admire in his first marketing plan for Vicks, as he conducted market research on horseback.

The company's new presentation to merchants described the

unusual ways VapoRub relieved symptoms of croupy cough without internal dosing. The mystery of menthol from Japan, the loving application of the ointment to the chest, and the hours-long relief by vapors gave salespeople the fuel for a dramatic sales talk that stressed consumer needs, particularly those of mothers who were frightened as they watched their children afflicted with croup struggle for breath.

The company offered 24 free jars with the purchase of a case so that the merchants could provide free samples. The company also began marketing through outdoor and in-store advertising. Smith Richardson was also a pioneer in the use of coupons, placing an ad that announced the product and included a coupon consumers could redeem at drugstores for free jars of VapoRub. Capitalizing on a U.S. Post Office regulation that allowed delivery to towns and RFD routes without naming the addressee (occupant mailings), the company was one of the first to begin an enormous sample-by-mail campaign throughout the western states.

Sales were climbing slowly.

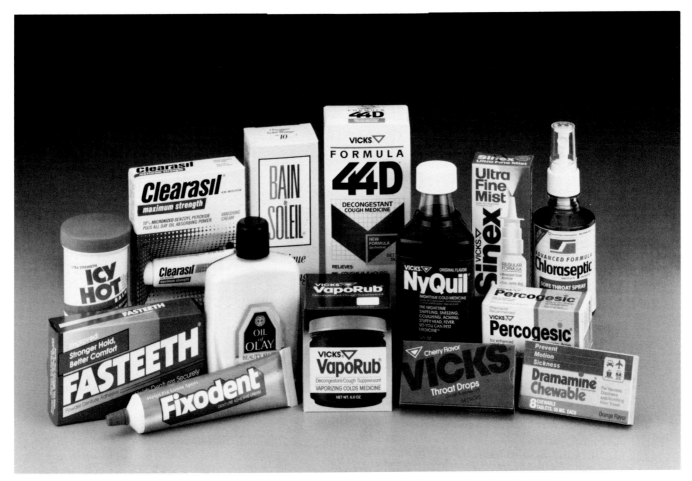

It all began with Vicks VapoRub, but today the Richardson-Vicks product line includes a wide range of well-known health and beauty care products.

Then came the great influenza epidemic of World War I. Lasting for more than one year, it sickened millions, and complications were often fatal.

Could Vicks VapoRub help? Before the epidemic, the company had the medical accuracy of its advertising reviewed by a prominent physician, which cleared the way for "how to" messages giving details on the history of influenza, symptoms, possible causes, avoidance, diet, and treatment, including use of VapoRub to ease difficult breathing. More than 17 million jars were sold that year, up from six million the year before.

The company's growth continued, due in part to Smith's determination to build an enduring business that would continue to satisfy consumers by understanding their needs and creating a climate to encourage innovation and give young people opportunities to grow into leadership positions.

In 1932 the Vick School of Applied Merchandising was formed to recruit outstanding college graduates into a rigorous two-year program combining sales, advertising assignments, and developmental positions at corporate headquarters. Today, as part of Procter & Gamble, Richardson-Vicks employees continue to benefit from this commitment to helping people develop to the best of their abilities.

Concern for satisfying consumer needs also led to expansion of the product line. Over the years, research efforts yielded such well-known products as Vicks Formula 44 cough medicines, Vicks Sinex decongestant nasal spray, and Vicks NyQuil. Diversification soon followed into personal care categories with Clearasil acne treatments, Fasteeth and Fixodent denture adhesives, Oil of Olay beauty fluid, and Bain de Soleil suncare products.

Behind each of these products, and the others yet to come from the Shelton labs, lies a company commitment to superior quality and value in the tradition of Lunsford and Smith Richardson.

The company's 75-acre site in Shelton is devoted to the development and marketing of new and better products to meet consumers' health and beauty care needs.

FORSCHNER GROUP, INC.

ing at 151 Long Hill Cross Roads, where the company continues to make inroads in its field, recently adding more Swiss Army brand products to its repertoire, including watches, compasses, and even sunglasses. The company also leases a warehouse facility in downtown Shelton.

Its professional cutlery products continue to expand, with a cata-

LEFT: In 1984 Forschner moved to this new corporate headquarters in Shelton.

BELOW: Forschner's huge Swiss factory building in Ibach is dwarfed by the awesome peaks which rise around it.

A crew of astronauts zoom off into space. A team of climbers ascend Mount Everest. Jacques Cousteau investigates the depths of the oceans. For such explorers, as well as for countless woodsmen, fishermen, and even city slickers, the Victorinox, the original Swiss Army Officer's Knife, serves as standard equipment—a virtual pocket tool box. The well-known gleaming red and silver knives, whose designs feature a distinguished cross within a shield, is exclusively marketed in the United States by the Forschner Group. Its principal executive offices are located in 151 Long Hill Cross Roads in Shelton.

Founded in 1855 as R.H. Forschner, a manufacturer of scales in New Britain, the firm moved to New York City in 1890. After World War I it began importing German cutlery. Prior to the next world war, the company began marketing Swiss-Victorinox cutlery, which, in addition to the Swiss Army Knife, included professional cutlery. Forschner ceased its scale manufacturing in 1957 to concentrate on the sale of Swiss cutlery for slaughterhouses.

In 1974 the firm was purchased by its current management with the

aim of focusing on the development of the Swiss Army Knife. In 1976 high taxes in New York City and state as well as the need for additional space prompted the company to move to Shelton, where it leased 25,000 square feet of office and warehouse space on Bridgeport Avenue. At the time of the move the firm had 22 employees.

By 1984 Forschner had outgrown even this space and moved to a new 24,000-square-foot office build-

log of items ranging from butcher knives to sharpening stones to spatulas and even ice chisels.

Today the company employs some 100 people, and, in a joint program, helps provide work for members of the Valley Association for Retarded Children and Adults, who help assemble boxed sets of knives, put labels on packages, and perform other tasks. The Forschner Group, Inc., also is active in supporting the Boys' Club of Shelton/Derby.

RAGÚ FOODS CO.

At Ragú Foods Co. headquarters in Trumbull, an artistic neon sculpture hangs in the lobby, flashing the name many American's think of when they think Italian—Ragú.

The sign provides an upbeat image for a progressive company; a firm that built its success on a traditional product—Ragú Old World Style Spaghetti Sauce—and went on

ABOVE: Since the first batch of Ragú sauce was made in 1937 in the kitchen of Giovanni and Assunta Cantisano, Ragú has created four different and delicious spaghetti sauce blends.

LEFT: Ragú also markets Adolph's marinades, seasonings, and tenderizers.

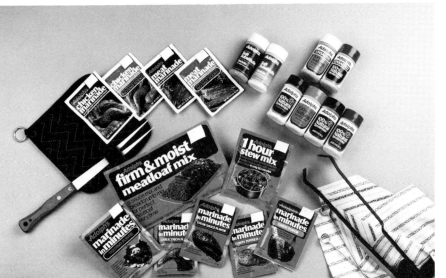

to claim a dominant share of the U.S. sauce market.

The first batch of Ragú, which translates as "sauce," was made in 1937 in the kitchen of Giovanni and Assunta Cantisano, immigrants who turned their family recipe into what eventually became a multimillion-dollar business. The sauce was sold door to door in the neighborhood until the Ragú Packing Company was founded in 1946 in Rochester. Acquired in 1969 by Chesebrough-Ponds, Ragú soon expanded beyond its northeast U.S. market region to become a household name in the kitchens of America. In 1973 Ragú became the first spaghetti sauce nationally available in grocery stores.

With its mild tomato flavor and blend of spices and cheese, Ragú Old World Style sold well in markets with a large Italian population. How-

ever, with the market growing 20 percent per year, it was evident consumers were also purchasing other types of sauces; a fact confirmed in 1976 when a competitor launched a new spaghetti sauce. In less than six months, Ragú responded with Ragú Extra Thick and Zesty, thicker than its original sauce and flavored with a zesty blend of spices, which soon gained a sizable share of the market. Other successful products followed: Ragú Homestyle, a sauce without sugar or corn syrup; Chunky Gardenstyle, a thicker sauce with a pulpier texture, containing chunks of vegetables; Thick and Hearty, a very thick sauce made from a special blend of herbs and spices in plain, mushroom, meat, and marinara varieties; and the newest introduction, Fresh Italian, a light, delicate, and fresh tasting sauce with extra tomatoes.

In 1981 Ragú also introduced a line of pizza sauces and homemade pizza crust. The company also markets Adolph's marinades, and tenderizers and has a food-service line of products where sauces and related products are offered in institutional sizes.

Operating since 1986 as an independent unit within Unilever, an international food and personal products conglomerate, Ragú maintains a research and development laboratory in Shelton where a team of scientists, engineers, technicians, and administrative staff spearheads the company's new product formulation, development, quality, and processing technology.

As Ragú continues to work within a large food company like Unilever, the opportunity for new product development is immense. Already the interchange of ideas and personnel has proved fruitful for both parties, with Ragú products being successfully launched in the United Kingdom, West Germany, Australia, and Canada. The future for Ragú Foods as part of Unilever looks promising as it is destined for success in new markets throughout the world.

FARREL CORPORATION

The history of Farrel Corporation reflects the changes and even the traumas of American manufacturing concerns as they struggle to remain viable businesses worthy of their beginnings.

The 150-year history of the Farrel Corporation is the story of two companies physically near to one another, established in Derby and Ansonia to more efficiently serve the growing industrialization of the Connecticut River valleys.

The Birmingham Iron Foundry in Derby (formerly known as Birmingham) and the Farrel Foundry &

ABOVE: This photo shows the Farrel Foundry & Machine Company circa 1863. The log-shaped castings in the yard are cannon barrels for use in the Civil War.

LEFT: The 18UMSD side-discharge, continuous mixer with melt pump and pelletizer for polyethylene production yields 70,000 pounds per hour.

Machine company in Ansonia were organized to manufacture machinery and equipment involved with the use of river water as a source of power for mills.

With a $5,000 investment, the Birmingham Iron Foundry was founded in 1836. The small foundry made castings, including water pipes and machinery for various types of mills. The Farrel Foundry & Machine company was founded in 1848 to produce iron parts for water power generation, which had up until that point been imported from out of state. The cash capital investment of $15,000 proved to be all of the cash capital

that was ever put into the business.

Both companies at first were only foundries. By the early 1850s, however, a small machine shop was built by Farrel for secondary operations. By that decade, too, both firms were making brass and iron parts from castings, machined with water-powered equipment, as well as roll mills and rubber processing machinery. By the late 1850s Farrel also found a ready market in the area of chilled iron rolls, that formerly had to be imported from England. The huge iron rolls are used in calenders to produce rubber sheet goods and other rubber products. The Farrel

version became not only the foundation for many of polymer processing products but also a product in its own right for more than 100 years.

In 1854 an order for rubber calenders was placed by Henry B. Goodyear, the brother of Charles Goodyear, who accidentally discovered the process of vulcanization of rubber in 1839. This led to the growth of the rubber industry and a subsequent need for equipment built by both Farrel Foundry & Machine and Birmingham Iron (although Birmingham did not have the foundry capabilities to produce chilled iron rolls).

During the Civil War, as during the first and second world wars, the company's production was diverted from peacetime products to the manufacture of war equipment.

In the 1870s Farrel Foundry & Machine Company began making a machine used for the grinding of sugar cane—Farrel soon became a leader in the field. It would take up

The 36-inch by 126-inch, "tilted," 4-roll, "z" type, calender produces a rubber-membrane roofing sheet 10 feet wide.

to 60 railroad freight cars to transport the machine to a port where it would fill the hold of an entire freighter headed for the West Indies. Installation would take one year.

In 1916 Birmingham employed inventor Fernley H. Banbury, designer of the Banbury Mixer® that revolutionized the processing of rubber, making earlier types of machines produced both by itself and by Farrel obsolete. In 1927 the two companies merged as Farrel-Birmingham Company, Incorporated. In the same decade a company in Buffalo that produced gears and gear units was acquired and, shortly after, the purchase of the American rights to the Sykes gear patents was arranged and Farrel-Sykes gears, gear units, and gear generators were manufactured in Buffalo. During World War II Farrel-Birmingham built propulsion gear units for more than 1,000 U.S. Navy and maritime commission ships.

In 1951 the firm acquired the consolidated Machine Tool Corporation of Rochester, that manufactured machine tools such as lathes, vertical and horizontal boring machines, and milling and planing machines. Five years later it purchased the assets of the press division of the Watson-Stillman Company, Division of H.K. Porter, which produced hydraulic presses for metal extrusion and plastic injection molding machines. Soon after, licensing arrangements were made for the manufacturing of Farrel design machinery in England, Italy, Australia, and then Japan and India.

In 1962 the company's name was changed to Farrel Corporation, and in 1966 the Farrel family sold the firm to USM Incorporated of Massachusetts, which was itself later purchased by Emhart of Hartford.

Prior to the mergers, the Buf-

falo plant was consolidated into the Rochester plant. Later, under the direction of Emhart, this plant was closed and some of its products transferred to the Valley. With increasing competition, the direction of the company was to consolidate, retrench, and downgrade, not only in its range of products but in the size and volume of business, which reached its lowest level in 1986, when Farrel once again became a private company as a result of a buyout, by a private investor, from Emhart.

The first objective of the new owner was to "turn the business around," focusing its attention on the marketplace, changing from a manufacturing-driven company to a market-driven one. Today the Farrel Corporation has once again returned the luster to the name of Farrel for the machinery it produces for the polymer processing industries of the world. The future holds much promise for this company of long heritage.

RAPP'S PARADISE INN

In the lobby of Rapp's Paradise Inn in Ansonia hangs a copy of the Rapp Family Tree, which dates back to 1665 and the birth of Christian Rapp, who operated an inn near Elzach in the Black Forest in Germany.

With such origins, it's no wonder his ancestors were to make restaurant history in the Naugatuck Valley. It all began in the United States with Adolph Lothar Rapp (popularly known as Otto) who immigrated to America at the age of four.

In 1896 he arrived in Derby to assist his father, Adolph Rapp, Sr., in the management of the Hoffman House, a well-known hostelry on Main Street that under his direction boasted the first amusement garden in the East.

Several years later Otto founded Rapp's Restaurant in Shelton. Married to Josephine Wagner in 1904, the couple had six children, five of whom became involved in their father's enterprises.

His eldest daughter, Madeline Conti, took over the ownership and management of Rapp's Restaurant, housed in a three-and-a-half story brick building. A Shelton landmark, it demoralized longtime customers when it burned to the ground on Thanksgiving of 1980, sometime after Conti sold it.

Son Robert Rapp took over the catering end of the family business and for a time also operated a canteen service in Valley factories. He now operates Rapp's Grassy Hill Lodge in Derby, used for banquets and outings.

Son Frank Rapp ran the Oxford house for a short period before World War II. After the war he worked for Conti until 1954, when he purchased Rapp's Paradise Inn, now known for its tasty beef, seafood, and chicken dishes and for its banquet and wedding facilities. It is also a frequent meeting place for business people and politicians.

Daughter Elizabeth St. Laurent and her husband Gerard worked for a time for Robert Rapp, and later had their own canteen service before they retired. The third daughter, Josephine Ledell, has enjoyed life outside the restaurant business. The late George Rapp also followed in the family footsteps, working as banquet manager of the Waldorf-Astoria.

Many of the third generation are also involved in the restaurant trade, including Patricia Reynolds, Frank's daughter, and her husband John, who manage Rapp's Paradise Inn; Joanne Rapp, who is following in her father Robert's footsteps along with her husband, Allan Holden; Elizabeth St. Laurent's son Gerard, Jr., who owns a prepared produce supply house in Texas, and her daughter Deborah, who operates Aruba Catering, which supplies all the food on airplanes leaving Aruba.

The Rapp siblings: (from left) Frank Rapp, Josephine Ledell, Madeline Conti, Robert Rapp, and Elizabeth St. Laurent.

AUTOSWAGE PRODUCTS INC.

What do chain and ball assemblies in toilet tanks, needles used to inflate footballs, spring guides for car door locks, printed circuit board pins, and hinge pins for eye shadow cases have in common? They are all items made by Autoswage Products Inc. on automatic die swaging equipment, used to produce highly intricate pin-shaped metal parts to precision tolerances at greatly reduced costs.

Among other things, the company also sells millions of key chains per year, as well as beaded chains used in time clocks, photocopier machines, musical instruments, toys, and even vertical blinds.

Also offering plating, pin rolling, fourslide, and stamping capabilities, the company has attracted a roster of more than 1000 customers in almost every imaginable type of business, with export sales to many foreign countries.

It all began in a small garage on Roberts Street in Shelton in 1946 as H.G.H. Products. Headed by the late Bart Hall, the firm experienced a steady growth, moving to the Star Pin Building on Canal Street in 1952, when it changed its name. The next move was to a leased building on Brook Street, and then, in 1966, the company built its own 28,000-square-foot building on River Road.

Two years later the firm acquired General Tool & Gauge, a fourslide manufacturing company in Wolcott. In 1977 the company had outgrown its space, and it purchased a 20,000-square-foot building in Beacon Falls, shutting down the Wolcott plant and incorporating its

operation as well as some departments from the Shelton plant into the new facility. Today almost all production is centered in Shelton, with the Beacon Falls facility expanded to 30,000 square feet serving as a warehouse.

The company was involved for a time in the 1980s with bandoliering square, pins called Wraposts™, first manufacturing them on die swaged bandoliering equipment and later acquiring a California company that produced bandoliered products using stamping technology. This product line and all supporting equipment has been sold.

Except for a period from 1968 to 1971 when the company was owned by a Florida-based mini-conglomerate, Autoswage has remained in the

RIGHT: Autoswage Products Inc., originally called H.G.H. Products, was founded by Bart Hall in 1946.

BELOW: The company began in a small garage on Robert Street in Shelton.

hands of the Hall family.

With annual sales averaging $12 to $13 million, Autoswage is involved in many dynamic growth industries, constantly seeking out new applications for its unique processes in order to maintain leadership in the field of automatic die swaging, die rolling, and beaded chain.

THE EVENING SENTINEL

Since 1871 *The Evening Sentinel* has never missed a day of publication. The presses never missed a beat during the blizzard of 1888, the hurricane of 1938, or the flood of 1955 (when the water level on Main Street reached heights of more than eight feet).

Even a fire in the pressroom in the 1970s failed to keep the paper from printing. One can only wonder if the Reverend E.M. Jerome of the First Baptist Church of Ansonia ever imagined he would be establishing such an institution when he launched the paper with M. Carpenter.

When it was founded, Ansonia was a borough of the town of Derby and the *Derby Transcript,* a weekly that was to cease publication in 1902, was the area's leading newspaper. Seymour, the next town to the north of Ansonia and a former part of Derby, had its own newspaper as well, the *Seymour Intelligencer.*

Reverend Jerome initially bought the Ansonia facilities of the *Transcript* and set up shop as a job printer. Since the equipment was already there, it is speculated, he could not resist the opportunity to publish a newspaper called, at the time, *The Naugatuck Valley Sentinel.* A weekly when it was established, it became a daily after five years.

On August 24, 1876, seven weeks after the United States celebrated its centennial, Reverend Jerome sold the newspaper to 30-year-old James Marion Emerson.

Emerson began his newspaper career working for his father, who was publisher and editor of the *American Union* in Denton, Maryland, a newspaper that unabashedly served as the area's Republican party spokesperson. After working several years there, he joined the staff of the Wilmington (Delaware) *Daily Commercial* before purchasing the *The Sentinel* along with another Wilmingtonian, W. Cramer, who sold out his share to Emerson within two years.

Emerson brought an energetic, aggressive leadership to his paper. Although staunchly Republican, he maintained an independent editorial policy and defended or attacked each issue on its merits, regardless of party affiliation. Under his guidance, circulation rose from 600 per weekly issue in 1876 to an average of 4,800 a day in 1900.

This fact was attested to on the front page of the January 2, 1901, edition. Joel S. Neal, a pressman, subscribed under oath that he printed 1,483,390 papers in the previous year. *The Sentinel* had the highest per capita circulation of any newspaper in the state. One of every six persons in its market area received the paper.

Emerson's editorial policy was to serve the community interest and to take sides when necessary. He strongly supported the borough in its successful fight to separate from Derby and to become a separate town, which took place in 1889.

Ansonia thrived as a manufacturing center and the newspaper along with it, soon changing its name to *The Ansonia Evening Sentinel.* It sold for two cents in stores and through home delivery and has been available since 1883 for delivery through mail. In 1884 Emerson added a special midweek section for the suburban areas that sold for three cents.

The newspaper became one of the earliest clients of the Associated Press, receiving telegraphic news reports from around the world by special wire every day up to the 4 p.m. printing time. In 1899 the newspaper acquired the first of five Morganthaler linotype machines, which eliminated cumbersome handset type, putting *The Evening Sentinel* once again in the forefront of Connecticut newspapers.

The newspaper was soon experiencing growing pains. It had already outgrown its quarters on the corner of Main and Maple streets, and the editorial house was staffed in the building next door. The former editorial room was transformed into the press room; the composing department was moved to the present site of the YMCA on State Street. To consolidate operations and allow for expansion, Emerson chose a building lot a little farther down Main Street, next to the lot on which the new city hall was to be built. Both buildings rose side by side and are still used by their original owners 86 years later.

In 1904 Connecticut newspapers founded an organization known as the Associated Dailies, with Emerson its first elected chairman. In April 1907 Emerson brought his two sons into the business and the company became the Emerson Publishing Co., with J.M. as president, Howard F. as first vice president, J. Ralph as second vice president, and F.N. Burr as treasurer. In 1922 the senior Emerson retired, turning the business over to his sons, who reincorporated it into Emerson Bros., Inc., and continued the family operation until it was sold by Susanne Wilmont, the founder's granddaughter, to the Thomson Newspapers of Des Plaines, Illinois, who has operated it since 1969.

Over the years much has changed in terms of design, style, and content, but the task set out by J.M. Emerson has remained the same: "Ansonia, Derby, Seymour, Shelton, Oxford and Beacon Falls, . . . the bailiwick over which *The Sentinel* keeps watch and ward."

The Evening Sentinel *carries on a 120-year publication tradition.*

TRUMBULL MARRIOTT

In the late 1970s several people of vision realized the Lower Naugatuck Valley was changing. With the projected meetings of the Merritt Parkway and Route 8, they projected the area would become the heart of the region, with arteries projecting to Waterbury and Hartford to the north, to New York to the south. More and more people would be driving on those roads. More and more people would need a place to rest, relax, have business conferences, and enjoy a fine meal at the end of a busy business day.

With companies such as General Electric and IBM arriving on the scene, it became more apparent that the area could support a world-class hotel. Developer David Mack pro-

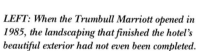

ABOVE: Guests can join the fun at Cahoots night-club if they are in the mood for a little nighttime entertainment.

LEFT: When the Trumbull Marriott opened in 1985, the landscaping that finished the hotel's beautiful exterior had not even been completed.

vided the leadership behind the move to attract a major business hotel, pointing to the some 2 million square feet of office and commercial space being developed in Fairfield county, with about 30 percent of it in the Valley.

As a result of his dedication and determination, the Trumbull Marriott was built. "I felt that it was the best hotel chain on the market," says Mack. "I feel it surpasses the other big name chains by leaps and bounds. It is the most consistent in terms of quality and service. You get the same high level of service in Trumbull as you would, for example, in our nation's capital."

The hotel, which opened in late 1985, is a joint venture between

Mack and the largest Marriott franchise. Primarily geared to the business traveler, the Trumbull Marriott has become known for its high level of service as well as its imaginative approach to meetings and conferences. Each group, for example, is assigned a personal executive meeting manager, one person whose sole responsibility is to handle every detail of the meeting.

The Trumbull Marriott features two specialized meeting packages that include complementary meeting room rentals and amenities, customized meeting room setups, catering concierge service, on-site audiovisual service, and flexible group rates for sleeping rooms.

Packages include such features

as a deli lunch or a constitution grille lunch and even a "Chocolate Energy" break with chewy fudge brownies, chocolate-chip cookies, chocolate-covered ice cream bars, and nonalcoholic liquid refreshments.

"Our goal," according to general manager Bob Andrews, "is to establish ourselves as the premier hotel operator in Fairfield County, if not in Connecticut."

Tastefully appointed by the interior design firm of Victor Huff Associates, the hotel captures a blend of visual drama and soothing color schemes.

For night excitement, there is the high-energy atmosphere of Cahoots nightclub, which features a Friday night "Dating Game," as well as its infamous "Blizzard of Bucks Box," a specially constructed glass case where air jets cause dollar bills to float, and guests occasionally get a

The hotel offers 321 elegant guest rooms (RIGHT) and suites (ABOVE) for the discriminating business traveler.

chance to "grab for the green."

For a romantic dinner for two or a sophisticated business supper, there is the elegant Ashley's restaurant. Gratzi, the seafood and pasta buffet restaurant, offers a setting for casual chic. For very special events there is the hotel's distinctive ballroom, offering more than 10,000 square feet that can also be subdivided for meeting purposes.

The hotel offers 321 guest rooms, a complete health club, as well as traditional hotel services, with more than 400 employees on staff,

all dedicated to attending to the needs of guests.

"We feel this hotel is an important link to the future of the area,"

says Andrews. "It gives area corporations a convenient location to extend hospitality in the grandest of style. We feel the influx of new businesses into the area the key to the hotel's continued success, particularly as it is situated at the confluence of four towns—Shelton, Stratford, Trumbull, and Bridgeport."

About 70 percent of the hotel's business is geared to the corporate customer who finds that, at the Trumbull Marriott, business is a pleasure.

WADS

Each weekend during football and basketball season, fans of the Valley high school teams know where to turn—to 690 AM, WADS, where they are able to tune in to the excitement and drama of the Ansonia Chargers, the Derby Red Raiders, the Seymour Wildcats, and the Shelton Gaels.

Established in the mid-1950s, the Ansonia-based station provides an enjoyable mix of music from the 1950s to the 1990s, as well as comprehensive coverage of high school sporting events and local news and weather. The 1,000-watt station is known for such features as trivia contests and "Walk Down Main Street," a talk show that provides a forum for everyone from politicians to psychics.

Brian Dow (ABOVE) and Jack Whitten (LEFT) are two of WADS' popular on-air personalities.

At the heart of WADS is its commitment of providing live, remote broadcasts, operating either from permanent lines established at each of the Valley teams' home fields or from cellular telephone lines. This allows the station the ability to broadcast at virtually a moment's notice at any location within the LINX service area, something that provides for greater versatility when covering local news, such as the River Restaurant explosion, or special events,

such as Olde Derby Day, as well as sporting events. If a game should be canceled at the last minute due to inclement weather or for other reasons, the station is able to broadcast another game simply by driving to the location.

The station typically offers coverage of Friday evening, Saturday afternoon, and Saturday evening games. Whenever possible it also offers coverage of the Notre Dame Green Knights of West Haven and

St. Joseph's Cadets in Trumbull, two schools that many Valley residents attend.

The station established its tradition of local coverage at the very beginning, when Syd Byrnes, who worked in the advertising department of a New York City radio station, approached David Schpero and his brother William, who lived in the Valley, about starting a radio station there. Such an operation did not previously exist, and residents typically listened to stations in other nearby cities.

Enlisting the aid of attorney Samuel Freed, public relations specialist Lee Eisenberg, as well as a group of investors, the men formed WADS with the permission of the FCC (Federal Communications Commission), establishing it first as a daytime station. The radio station was sold several times, and it is currently owned by Manuel Santos. It operates from 6 a.m. to 10 p.m., providing Valley residents with hour after hour of entertainment, sports, news, and weather.

BROWNING-FERRIS INDUSTRIES, INC.

The Browning-Ferris blue truck is a familiar site on Naugatuck Valley roads, carting away waste products from homes, businesses, hospitals, and industries.

As its wheels lap up the miles, Valley residents can be assured that it represents a company committed to responsible collection and disposal of commercial, residential, and municipal solid waste and industrial hazardous wastes.

The Derby District office offers no exception to Browning-Ferris Industries' exemplary track record nationwide. Founded in the mid-1960s as W.R. Archer & Co., the facility has tripled in size since 1984, when it was acquired by BFI. Such expansion required the building of a new office on a seven-acre site on Derby Avenue in Seymour.

A variety of services are provided through the Derby district. BFI provides residential pickup for the cities of Ansonia, Derby, and Shelton as well as transfer station operation for the town of Seymour and several Connecticut communities.

It also provides solid waste col-

Browning-Ferris Industries has tripled in size since 1984 and has expanded to a new office on a seven-acre site in Seymour.

lection for commercial accounts ranging from small mom-and-pop shops to large factories, as well as medical waste disposal for St. Vincent and Park City Hospitals in Bridgeport and a number of doctors' offices statewide. The company offers special seminars for appropriate personnel offering specialized data and support in this sensitive area. Recently the director of plant operations at Park City Hospital wrote, "It is gratifying to know that BFI stands for quality information and unsurpassed service of its accounts in the area of regulated medical wastes."

Another focus of the BFI Derby District is a new business started in January—the supplying of portable toilets throughout the lower half of the state to construction sites, festivals, outdoor concerts, and other events.

The Derby District has also led the way in the company's recycling

arena. Working far ahead of the January 1, 1991, date set by the Connecticut legislature as the day that 25 percent of the total waste stream in the state be recycled and that all municipalities implement appropriate programs, BFI has provided a program for commercial customers to separate clean corrugated cardboard for delivery to a paper mill in Waterbury and will be expanding its service to its customers to include other mandated recycling items.

BFI's mission is to provide the highest quality waste collection, transport, processing, disposal, and related services to both public and private customers worldwide. BFI will carry out their mission efficiently, safely, and in an environmentally responsible manner with respect for the role of government in protecting the public interest.

BFI is also aggressively responding to municipal curb-side collection programs and will assist communities in educating residents on proper procedures for recycling. Drop-off centers are also under consideration.

RESIDENCE INN BY MARRIOTT

There's no place like home. Except, of course, the Residence Inn by Marriott in Shelton, which serves as a home on the road for business travelers.

People who travel for a living "live" at the the Residence Inn, housed in many major cities, including Shelton—located in the midst of a corporate belt that boasts the company of such firms as Sikorsky, IBM, Philips Medical, Richardson-Vicks, and Pitney Bowes.

The hotels are designed to resemble a condominium complex, clustered within a neighborhood-like setting. Attractive, low-rise town houses have beautifully landscaped walkways and private entrances. Inside, the comforts of home continue in spacious, yet intimate studio suites that are 50 percent larger than typical hotel rooms and offer separate sleeping and living areas and a full-size, fully equipped kitchen.

Two-story penthouse suites are also available, with enough versatility and privacy for two people or a family. The two levels have two sleeping areas, two full bathrooms, two closets, and even two televisions.

The Residence Inn offers the perfect ending to the business day, with room for unwinding at its pool, heated spa, racquet sports, basketball, and volleyball courts. Or, for homebodies, there might be a cozy night ahead in front of a fireplace, available in most rooms.

The average length of stay at the Residence Inn-Shelton is 10 days, with some travelers staying up to a month or more. In order to foster a sense of community, the management offers a hospitality hour on Monday through Thursday nights, from 5:30 to 7:00 p.m.

At these gatherings free beer, wine, and soft drinks are offered along with a light hot meal, often with a party theme. When a group of members of the Australian Royal Navy

were staying at the Inn, for example, the management sponsored a special Australian night with Fosters Beer from Australia, along with Australian food. In addition, a complementary continental breakfast and free newspaper are offered each day.

At such gatherings, guests are likely to find themselves meeting business travelers from Japan, Europe, Russia, or other foreigners who have come to learn that the Residence Inn translates into comfort in any language.

While the inn strives to be a home away from home, its business is also business. The friendly staff will help take care of all professional needs—from arranging transportation, secretarial services, meeting rooms, and catering. They will recommend area restaurants and sight-seeing attractions.

Some might say Residence Inn by Marriott is an idea whose time has come. Some four years ago it became very obvious to area developers that

ABOVE: The Residence Inn combines the intimacy of a bed and breakfast with the professional service and convenience of a fine hotel.

BELOW: The Residence Inn hotel is designed to resemble a neighborhood-like condominium complex.

Shelton was fast becoming an up and coming city—that the long arm of expansion of corporate America from New York City to Stamford was continuing on a bee line to Shelton.

Corporate parks provide a natural attraction for Residence Inn, drawing on their large base of corporate travelers, providing them with something unique, restful, and dif-

The attractive town houses have beautifully landscaped walkways and private entrances.

agement, filling an obvious, but until now, overlooked niche—providing quarters for business travelers with the intimacy of a bed and breakfast and the professional polish and conveniences of a hotel chain.

The management is eminently accessible, "bending over backwards" to provide everything from directions to a business meeting to handling medical or other emergency situations. They will also make sure guests are provided with free transportation to and from airports and train stations.

And the management makes it easy to make oneself at home with prices that are comparable to moderate-price hotel rooms and rates that reward the traveler for longer stays. The Marriott Residence Inn Company is the leader in extended-stay lodging.

ferent. Today the Residence Inn by Marriott-Shelton services the Enterprise Corporate Park, the Armstrong Corporate Park, and the busy Bridgeport Avenue section, as well as several other large corporate parks located within the immediate area.

Business has been bustling at the Residence Inn, exceeding the expectations and predictions of man-

LEFT: The suites are much larger than typical hotel rooms and offer separate, spacious sleeping and living areas as well as fully equipped kitchens.

BELOW: The complex's two-story penthouse suites offer two sleeping areas, two full bathrooms, two closets, two television sets, and enough versatility and privacy for two people.

Patrons

The following individuals, companies, and organizations have made a valuable commitment to the quality of this publication. Windsor Publications and the Lower Naugatuck Valley Chamber of Commerce gratefully acknowledge their participation in *The Lower Naugatuck Valley: A Rich and Beautiful Prospect.*

Autoswage Products Inc.*
W.E. Bassett Company*
Brennan Construction Company*
Browning-Ferris Industries, Inc.*
Curtiss-Ryan, Inc.*
Derby Savings Bank*
The Evening Sentinel*
Farrel Corporation*
Forschner Group, Inc.*
Great Country Bank*
Griffin Hospital*
Hershey Metal Products, Inc.*
Petrol Plus*
Ragú Foods Co.*
Rapp's Paradise Inn*
Residence Inn by Marriott*
Richardson-Vicks*
Summagraphics Corporation*
Tetley Inc.*
Trumbull Marriott*
Valley Cable Vision, Inc.*
WADS*

*Partners in Progress of *The Lower Naugatuck Valley: A Rich and Beautiful Prospect.* The histories of these companies and organizations appear in Chapter 8, beginning on page 87.

Huntington remained the most rural of the developing Naugatuck Valley towns during the first half of the nineteenth century, and the classic Federal architecture of this period is reflected in the doorway of the Marks-Brownson House, the current home of the Huntington Historical Society. The semi-eliptical fanlight above the door is adorned with leaded festoons, rosettes, and the American eagle. The dentil molding on the porch and the beading above the fanlight also reflect the style of the Federal period. Courtesy, Jeanette LaMacchia

Bibliography

Papers, letters, articles, and documents at the Derby Public Library, the Connecticut State Library, the Connecticut Historical Society, New Haven Colony Historical Society, Derby Historical Society, New Haven Public Library, Yale University libraries, Wesleyan University Library, and Bridgeport Public Library were valuable in the research for this book.

Also of great value were the bound volumes and microfilms of the region's newspapers: *The Derby Journal, The Evening Sentinel, The Seymour Record, New Haven Register, Connecticut Journal, New Haven Palladium, Bridgeport Evening Standard, Bridgeport Herald, Waterbury American.*

Books and journals used included:

Ancient Town Records of New Haven. New Haven Colony Historical Society. New Haven: 1917.

Andrews, William G. *The Trading House on the Paugasset.* Papers of the New Haven Colony Historical Society. Vol. IV. New Haven: 1888.

A Pictorial History of Shelton, Connecticut. Gettysburg, Pa.: 1987.

A Walloon Family in America: Lockwood DeForest and His Forbears. Boston: 1914.

Baldwin, Charles G. *The Baldwin Genealogy.* Cleveland: 1881.

Barron, Milton L. *People Who Intermarry: Intermarriage in a New England Industrial Community.* Syracuse, N.Y.: 1946.

Beardsley, E. Edwards. *History of the Episcopal Church in Connecticut.* New York: 1874.

Byrne, William, editor. *History of the Catholic Church in New England.* Vol. II. Boston: 1899.

Campbell, Hollis A., William C. Sharpe and Frank G. Bassett. *Seymour, Past and Present.* Seymour: 1902.

Clark, Frederick P. and Associates. *The Naugatuck Valley Region: A Regional Planning Study of Conditions and Prospects, 1955-1957.* Rye, N.Y.: 1957.

Coffin, C.C. "An Indian Village Site at Cedar Ridge, Upper White Hills, Shelton, Connecticut." Bulletin of the Archaeological Society of Connecticut. November, 1938.

Danensberg, Elsie N. *Naval History of Fairfield County Men in the Revolution.* Stratford, Connecticut: 1977.

DeForest, John W. *History of the Indians of Connecticut From the Earliest Known Period to 1850.* Hamden, Connecticut: 1964.

Derby Savings Bank 1846-1946. Derby: 1946.

Dexter, Franklin Bowditch, editor. *The Literary Diary of Ezra Stiles.* New York: 1901.

Dwight, Timothy. *Travels in New England and New York.* Cambridge, Mass.: 1969.

Early Houses of Oxford. Historic House Committee of the Bicentennial Commission. Derby: 1976.

Favretti, Rudy J. *Highlights of Connecticut Agriculture.* Storrs, Connecticut: 1976.

Fourteenth Annual Report of the Connecticut Bureau of Labor Statistics. Norwich, Connecticut: 1898.

Gillespie, C.B., illustrator and compiler. *Souvenir History of Derby and Shelton, Connecticut.* Issued by The Evening Transcript. Derby: 1896.

Hawkins, Ernest. *Historical Notices of the Missions of the Church of England in the North American Colonies.* London: 1845.

Hawks, Francis L. and William Stevens Perry. *Documentary History of the Protestant Episcopal Church in Connecticut.* Hartford: 1959.

Historical Record of the First Congregational Church, Derby, Connecticut.

Derby: 1920.

Hoadley, Charles J. *Public Records of the Colony of Connecticut.* Hartford: 1880.

Kelly, J. Frederick. *Early Connecticut Meetinghouses, Being an Account of the Church Edifices Built Before 1850 Based Chiefly Upon Town and Parish Records.* Two volumes. New York: 1948.

Larson, Dorothy A., editor. *A History of Ansonia.* New Haven: 1976.

Lathrop, William G. *The Brass Industry in the United States.* New Haven: 1926.

Lavin, Lucianne and Bert Salwen. "The Fastener Site: A New Look at the Archaic-Woodland Transition in the Lower Naugatuck Valley." Bulletin of the Archaeological Society of Connecticut. 1983.

Litchfield, Norman and Sabina Connolly. *History of the Town of Oxford, Connecticut.* Oxford: 1960.

Marcus, Jacob R. *The Colonial American Jew.* Two volumes. Detroit: 1970.

McMullen, Ann. "Tribal Style in Woodsplint Basketry: Early Paugusset Influence." Artifacts, Vol. XI, No. 4. Washington, Connecticut: 1983.

Molloy, Leo T., compiler. *Tercentenary Pictorial and History of the Lower Naugatuck Valley.* Ansonia: 1935.

Nichols, Charles. *Autobiography of Rev. Charles Nichols in a Series of Letters to His Granddaughter.* New Britain: 1881.

O'Mara, Kevin. *Valley Downtowns: A Historical Perspective.* Derby: 1980.

Orcutt, Samuel. *A History of the Old Town of Stratford and the City of Bridgeport, Connecticut.* New Haven: 1886.

—————. *The Indians of the Housatonic and Naugatuck Valley.*

Stamford, Connecticut: 1972.

———— and Ambrose Beardsley. *The History of the Old Town of Derby, Connecticut, 1642-1880.* Springfield, Mass.: 1880.

Osterweis, Rolin G. *Three Centuries of New Haven.* New Haven: 1953.

Pease, John C. and John M. Niles. *A Gazetteer of the States of Connecticut and Rhode Island.* Hartford: 1819.

Perry, William S. *The History of the American Episcopal Church 1587-1883.* Two volumes. Boston: 1885.

Phillips, Nancy O., compiler. *Town Records of Derby, Connecticut, 1655-1710.* New Haven: 1901.

"Report of the Banking Committee to the General Assembly." Hartford: 1855.

"Report of the Connecticut Flood Recovery Committee to Governor Abraham Ribicoff." Hartford: 1955.

Roberts, Gary B. *Genealogies of Connecticut Families.* Volume III. Baltimore: 1983.

Rockey, J.L., editor. *History of New Haven County, Connecticut.* Two volumes. New York: 1892.

Roth, Matthew. *Connecticut: An Inventory of Historic Engineering and Industrial Sites.* Washington, D.C.: 1981.

Salter, L.A., Jr. and H.S. Darling. "Part-Time Farming in Connecticut: A Socio-Economic Study of the Lower Naugatuck Valley." Storrs Agricultural Experiment Station, Bulletin 201. Storrs: 1935.

Scott, Kenneth. *Counterfeiting in Colonial America.* New York: 1957.

———— and Roseanne Conway. *Genealogical Data From Colonial New Haven Newspapers.* Baltimore: 1979.

"Seventeenth Annual Report of the Connecticut Bureau of Labor Statistics." Meriden: 1901.

Sharpe, William C. *History of Oxford.* Seymour:1885.

————. *Annals of the Seymour Methodist Episcopal Church.* Seymour: 1896.

Shelton, Jane De Forest. "The New England Negro, A Remnant." Harper's New Monthly Magazine. March 1894.

————. *The Salt-Box House, Eighteenth Century Life in a New England Hill Town.* New York: 1900.

Sherwood, Albert F. *Memories of Old Derby.* New Haven: 1924.

Stivers, Mabel P. *Lineage of Albert L. Johnson.*

Storrs, John W. *The Twentieth Connecticut, A Regimental History.* Ansonia: 1886.

Sturtevant, William C. *Handbook of North American Indians.* Vol. 15. Washington, D.C.: 1978.

Swigart, Edmund K. *The Prehistory of the Indians of Western Connecticut.* Washington, Connecticut: 1974.

The Birmingham National Bank of Derby, Connecticut, The First Hundred Years, 1848-1948. Derby: 1948.

The Future of Local Government in the Lower Naugatuck Valley. Institute of Public Service, University of Connecticut. Storrs: 1969.

The Historical, Statistical and Industrial Review of the State of Connecticut. New York: 1883.

"The Valley of the Naugatuck." The National Magazine. January 1858.

Townshend, Charles H. "Early History of Long Island Sound and Its Approaches." Papers of the New Haven Colony Historical Society. Vol. V. New Haven: 1894.

Trumbull, J. Hammond. *Indian Names of Places, Etc. in and on the Borders of Connecticut With Interpretations of Some of Them.* Hartford: 1881.

Trumbull, J. Hammond, editor. *Public Records of the Colony of Connecticut.* Hartford: 1852.

Wakeman, Robert P. *Wakeman Genealogy.* Meriden, Connecticut: 1900.

Wallace, John, *Genealogy of the Riggs Family.* NewYork: 1901

Whitefield's Journals. London: 1960.

White Hills of Shelton. Essex, Conn.

Wilcoxson, William H. *History of Stratford.* Bridgeport: 1939.

Wojciechowski, Franz L. *The Paugussett Tribe.* Nijmegen, The Netherlands: 1985.

Woodward, Joseph Gurley. *Currency and Banking in Connecticut.* Boston: 1896.

Wooster, Eugene R. *The Edward Wooster Family.* 1970.

Index

PARTNERS IN PROGRESS INDEX
Autoswage Products Inc., 113
Bassett Company, W.E., 89
Brennan Construction Company, 95
Browning-Ferris Industries, Inc., 119
Curtiss-Ryan, Inc., 94
Derby Savings Bank, 96-97
The Evening Sentinel, 114-115
Farrel Corporation, 110-111
Forschner Group, Inc., 108
Great Country Bank, 92-93
Griffin Hospital, 90-91
Hershey Metal Products, Inc., 98-99
Lower Naugatuck Valley Chamber of
    Commerce, 88
Petrol Plus, 101
Ragú Foods Co., 109
Rapp's Paradise Inn, 112
Residence Inn by Marriott, 120-121
Richardson-Vicks, 106-107
Summagraphics Corporation, 100
Tetley Inc., 104-105
Trumbull Marriott, 116-117
Valley Cable Vision, Inc., 102-103
WADS, 118

GENERAL INDEX
Italicized numbers indicate illus-
trations.

A
Academy Hill, 85
Acadians, 30; refugees, 32
Adams, Samuel, 27-28
African-Americans, 24, 34, 44, 53-54
Ajello, Carl, 83
Alling Mills, *41*
Allis, George C., 50
American Brass Co., 60
American Brass Co. bridge, 70
Americanization of immigrants, 63
Anglican Church, *25*
Ansonia, 42; city hall, *66;* Cliff Street,
    85; Memorial Day Parade, *58;*
    town status of, 55-56
Ansonia Clock Company, *44*
Ansonia Copper and Brass Co., 85
Ansonia High School football, *82,* 83
Ansonia Nature Center, *85*
Ansonia Opera House, 50
Ansonia Savings Bank, 47
Arlington Hotel, 70

Arnold, Reverend Jonathon, 23
Auto Express Co., 60
Automobiles, first, 60, *61, 86*

B
Bacon, Jabez, 34-35
Baldwin, Richard, 13-15, 16, *16*
Baldwin, Eli N., Stump Joint Factory,
    22
Bartheleme, Claude, 30
Bartholomew, Claudius, 39, 40
Bartholomcw, Dana, 50
Baseball, 49
Bassett, R.W., Company, 52, *53*
"Battle Row," 61
Beacon Falls, 25, 47
Beacon Falls Center, *52*
Beardsley, Ambrose, 20, 55
Beecher, F.H., 60
Bicycle, first, 49
Birmingham Brass facility, 60
Birmingham High School, *56*
Birmingham Iron Foundry, *41, 54*
Blacklatch, Joseph, 27-28
Blakeman, James, 20
Block, Adrian, 11, 14
Boone, Maude, *64*
Booth, Stephen, 42
Bowen, William, 62
Bowers, Reverend John, 17, 22
Bowers, Samuel, 85
Bracci, Evo, 67
Branford Trolley Museum, 68
Branson Cleaning Equipment, 82
Brewster, Charles B., 60
Bridge Street (Shelton), 52, *53*
Brinsmade, D.S., 71
Bronson, Homer D., 60
Brownie Castle, 85
Brownson, Harry, 75
Brownson Country Club Golf
    Course, *75*
Bruenig, Eleanor, *66*
Bubar, David, 72, 81
Buckley, E.J., 53
Burwell, John, 13-14
Busoske, Joseph, 57

C
Capitol Theater, 64, 70
Carle, Alice, *66*
Carroll, James, 49

Cartier, Inc., 82
Carver, Warren, 66
Catholic Daughters of America, *66*
Cemetery Ridge battle, 49
Center School, 77
Charters, Stephen, 59, *60*
Church of England, 23, 25
Churma, Michael, 67
Civil War, 48-49
Clapham, Thomas, 36
Clark, David, 40
Clark, William, 31, 33
Coe, John A., 60
Coe, Truman, 44, 85
Coffee, William, 81
Comcowich, John, 67
Concordia Singing Society, 61
Congregational Church, *25*
Conklin, Henry, *65*
Connecticut Circle magazine, 66
Connecticut Fifth Regiment, *84*
Connecticut Gazette, 69
Connecticut Industry magazine, 66
Copperheads, 48
Corsell, William, 21
Crofut, Louise B., 60
Cryshie, Thomas, 53
Curtiss building, 52, *53*

D
Data Switch, 82
Daughters of the American Revolu-
    tion, 61
Davenport, Reverend James, 27
Davenport, Reverend John, 11
Davis, John, 34
Dayton, Ebenezer, 38
Dayton, Phoebe, 38
DeCapua, Vincent, 67
Derby: City Hall, 57; Derby Day Festi-
    val, 85; early shipping, *24;* electric
    street railroad, 57, *57;* establish-
    ment of, 13-17; first gristmill, 20;
    in 1845, 42-43
Derby Bank, 39
Derby Fishing Company, 38-39
Derby Historical Society, 84
Derby Journal, 43, 47, 53, 69
Derby Savings Bank, 47
Derby-Shelton Board of Trade, 65-66
Derby Silver Co., 52, *53,* 54, 78
Derby Temperance Society, 45

Derby Transcript, 50, 51, 56
Derby Wide Awakes, 48
Diamond Match Co., 85
DiMauro, Robert, 70-71
Donato, Anthony, *65*
Doyle, Joseph, 71
Durand, John, 24
Dutch, 11, 12; fur trading, *8*
Dutch Door Inn, 70
Dwight, Timothy, 9, 10, 85

E
Eaton, Theophilous, 11, 12-13
Edwards, Jonathon, *28*
Electric freight locomotive, first, *68*
Ellis, Thomas, 43
Emerson, Charles, 67
Emery, E.H., 82
English, 11, 13, 19, 30
Episcopal Glebe House Rectory, *35*
Ericson, Ethel, 65
Ericson, George T., 40
Evening Sentinel, 59, 61, 63, 64, 65,
    66, 67, 69

F
Farrel, Almon, 43
Farrel-Birmingham, 66
Farrel Foundry and Machinery Co.,
    59, 60, 85
Finnucan, Elizabeth, *66*
First Congregational Church
    (Derby), 85
First Regiment of Connecticut, *49*
Fishing, 21, 38-39, 42
Fitzpatrick, E.J., 62
Floods: (1767), 69; (1847), 69;
    (1891), 69, *70;* (1955), 69-71, *71*
Football mania, 83
Fountain Lake Commerce Park, 82
Fournier, Emil J., 62
Freeman, Jethro, 34
Freeman, Nancy, 44
Freeman, Roswell, 44
French and Indian War, 29, 30, 33

G
Gardner, John B., 53
Gavin, Robert, 67
Germans, 47
Gilyard, Thomas, 43
Gompers, Samuel, 59

Goodman, B., 53
Goodrich, B.F., Co., 72
Gorham, Joseph, 24-25
Grant, Daniel, 31
Great Awakening, the, 27-29
Great Depression, 64-66
Greek Catholic Ss. Peter and Paul
    Church, 61
Griffin Hospital, 64; *65*

H
Hallock shipyards, 36
Hart, Anna M. (Anna M. Hull), *40,*
    41
Hassard sisters, 53
Hatchett, Molly, 38
Hawkins, Joseph, 69
Healey, Henry, 67, *67*
Heavy industry, decline of, 81
High Rock Grove, 51
High-tech industrial boom, 81-82
Highways, 81-82
*History of the Old Town of Derby, Con-
    necticut, 1642-1880,* 55
Holbrook, Abigail, 23
Holbrook, Daniel, 37
Holbrook, John, 23
Holbrook, Josiah, 85
Holbrook Street School, 64
Holden, Reverend F.A., 61
Holmes, William, florist, 52, *53*
Home Woolen Mill, *45,* 84-85
Hopkins, Samuel, 13-14
Housatonic Power Plant, 52
Housatonic River, 51, 80
House of Hope, 11
Howe, John, 83
Howe Pin Co., 59
Hubbell, Clarence, 67
Hubbell industrial park, 82
Huguenots, 24
Hull, Isaac, 40, *40,* 41
Hull, John, 20
Hull, Joseph, 34
Hull, Samuel, 20
Hull, William, 33-34
Humphreys, Reverend Daniel, 28-29
Humphreys, David, *26, 35, 37, 38,* 49
Humphreys, Sarah Riggs, 61
Humphreys House, *84*
Humphreysville, 37, 38
Huntington, Samuel, *39*

Huntington, 39; independence of,
    38; in 1845, 42
Huntington Congregational Church,
    61
Huntington Green, *80, 83*
Huntington Historical Society, *122*
Hurricane Connie, 69
Hurricane Diane, 69

I
Ideal Manufacturing Co., 85
Immigrants, early twentieth century,
    60-62
Impellitteri, Vincent, *65, 66*
Indian Wells State Park, 80, 85
Indian Well waterfall, 22
Irish, 47-48, 63-64
Irving School, *56*
ITT, 82

J
James, Reverend John, 22
Jefferson, Thomas, 37, 39
Jews, 24, 63
Johnson, Ebenezer, 21, 24
Johnson, Nathaniel, 33
Jones' Tree Farm, *76*
Judson, Joseph, 16

K
Karlins, Maurice, 70
Kellogg, Elisha S., 49
Kellogg Environmental Center, *78*
Kennedy, William, *66*
Kieft, William, 12
Kinneytown Dam, 57
King George's War, 29
King Philip's War, 21, 23
Knights of Labor, 54-55
Know-Nothing party, 47
Kobasa, Tina and Stephen, 78
Kordiak, Stephen, 81
Kriz, Joseph, 67

L
Lake Housatonic, 85
Lallement, Pierre, 49, 51
LaMacchia, Dominick, family, *63*
Langdon, Edward, 13
Latex Foam Products, Inc., 81
Laurel Ledge elementary school, *83*
Leavenworth, Gideon, 38

Leavenworth, Thomas, 20
Lee, Reverend Jonathon, 29
Limburner, John, 43
Lombardi, Giovanni, 60
Long Island Sound, *12*
Lower Naugatuck Valley Chamber of Commerce, 82
Lyons, Reverend James, 23-24

M
MacArthur, Douglas, *66*
Macedonia Baptist Church, 85
Maltby, E.C., Company, 52, *53*
Mansfield, Anna, 35
Mansfield, Reverend Richard, 32, *34*
Manufacturer's Bank, 47
Maple Street Bridge, *71*
Marasco, Angelo, 67
Marks, Mordecai, 24
Marks-Brownson House, *122*
Marshall, Jim, 53
Martin, Jethro, 34
Martinez, A., 53
Martino, Nicholas, 70
Matthies, Ethel Clark, 78
Matthies, Bernard, 78
Matthies, Bernard H., Memorial Park, *78-79*
McCarthy, Anna, *66*
McElroy, Charles J., *62*
Metacom, King Philip, *23*
Methodist Episcopal Church, 59
Miles, Jonathon, 32
Milford, founding of, 11
Milford Beach, *55*
Mills, Reverend Jedidiah, 22, 27, 28, 29, 31, 33, 83
Minor, William T., 47-48
Modesty schooner, *36*
Moeller, Charles, 72, 81
Morgan, J. Pierpont, 75
Moshier's Hotel, 44-45
Murray, John R., 53
Mutual Aid, Inc., 65

N
Native Americans, 9, 11, 13, 25; Paugussetts, 10, 12, *13;* slavery, 24-25
Nature Center (Ansonia), 85
Naugatuck Forest, 85
Naugatuck Railroad, 47

Naugatuck steamboat, 42
Naugatuck Transportation Company, 42, 43
Naugatuck Valley Steamboat Company, 68
Navarro, Mrs. John, 69
New Deal programs, 65
New Haven, founding of, 11-12
New Haven Palladium, 44, 57
New Haven Register, 50-51, 53-54
New Haven Union, 55
Newson, Thomas M., 43
Nichols, Reverend Charles, 39
Nichols, Fred, *65*
Nitsuko America Corp., 82
Nolan, Andrew, *66*
Norwood Hall, 60

O
O'Brien, Emmett, Regional Vocational Technical School, 82
Ocain, Jeremiah, 31, 33
O'Donnell, George, 70
Old Yellow Mills, 20
O'Neill, William A., 82
Onrust ship, *14*
Orcutt, Samuel, 55
Osborne, John W., 43-44
Osbornedale State Park, 76
Osborne Homestead Museum, *76*
Osborne-Kellogg, Frances, 76
Ousatonic Dam, 52, 69, *71*
Oxford: independence of, 38; in 1845, 42; Olde Tyme Fair, *77*, 85
Oxford Airport, 82
Oxford Turnpike Company, 38

P
Paradyne Corp., 82
Paugussett Mills, 59
Pawlak, Michael, 67
Peck, E.W., stove and tinware shop, 52, *53*
People's Savings Bank, 47
Pero, Tobias, 34
Phelps, Anson, 57
Phelps, Anson, factory, 43
Philips Medical Systems, 82
Pierpont Block, *75*
Pine's bridge, *52*
Pinto, Abraham, 24
Plastic Molding Technology, 82

Pomeroy, Reverend Benjamin, 28
Population (1709), 21
Pork Hollow, 35
Pritchard, Jabez, 33
Puritan Church, 25
Puritans, 11
Putnam, Israel, 30

Q
Quaker Farms, *75,* 85
Quash, 34

R
Regional cooperation, 82-83
Religion, 22-24, 27-29, 85
Revolutionary War, 31-35
Richardson-Merrell, 82
Riggs, D.H., 60
Riggs, Edward, 13-14
Riggs, Samuel, 21
Rimmon Schoolhouse, 85
Rock Rimmon, *21*
Route 8, 81-82, *81,* 85
Rowell, David B., 48
Rubber Shoe Company, 45
Russell, Charles, 48

S
St. James Episcopal Church (Derby), 85
St. Mary's Catholic Church, *62,* 85
Ss. Peter and Paul Ukrainian Catholic Church, 85
Sanford, Thomas, 40
Schultz, Herman, 60
Seymour: industrial boom, 82; Pumpkin Festival, 85
Seymour High School, 70
Seymour Manufacturing Co., 66
Seymour Products Co., 66
Shaw, John H., 53
Shelton, Daniel, 23
Shelton, Edward N., 42
Shelton, Jane DeForest, 20, 31
Shelton, 9, 24; industrial boom, 82
Shelton High School, 81
Shelton settlement (Native American), 9-10, *11*
Sherwood, Albert, 19
Shipbuilding, 36
Silvermine industrial park, 82
Skowronski, Raymond, 61

Smith, Sheldon, 40-41
Smith, William N., 60
Southford Falls State Park, 85
Sperry, Walter, 56
Sponge Rubber Co., 66; explosion, 72, *72*, 81
Sports, 64
S&S Enterprises, 84
Stamford paddleboat, *43*
Stauffer Chemical Co., 82
Steele, Bradford, 33
Sterling Opera House, 83
Stevenson Dam, 85
Stratford, founding of, 11
Summagraphics, Inc., 82
Swirsky, Sam, *65*

T
Taylor, George Lansing, 48
Terell, Wales, 48-49
Tetley Tea, 82
Thompson, Jabez, 33
Three Saints Orthodox Church, 85
Thurston, Alfred, *65*
Tiano, John, 67
TIE Communications, Inc., 82
Titharton, Timothy, 20, 23
Toby (Native American slave), 25
Toby's Rock, 25
Tomlinson, Isaac, 34-35, 39
Tomlinson, Samuel, 31
Trapano's Savoia Band, 61
Tree, Reverend E.O., 59
Tucker, Daniel, 31, 33

U
Ukrainian Youth Organization, 66
University of Connecticut's Institute for Public Service unification study, 83
Union Cemetery, 70
Upson, Hiram, *50*

V
Valley Association for Retarded Children and Adults, 82
Valley Industrial Museum, 84
Valley Regional Planning Agency, 82
Valley Transit District, 82
Valley United Fund, 82
Van der Donck, Adrian, 11

Vartelas Block tenement, 70
Voccia, Vito, 67

W
Wakeman, John, 11-12, 15
Wallace, Thomas, 46
Wallace, William, 53
Wallace and Sons, 53
Waniga, Peter, 70, 71
War of 1812, 39-40
Washborn, Gideon, 31, 33
Washington, George, 26, 35
Washington Bridge, 39
Weed, Samuel, 31, 33
Weston, Juba, 44
Weston, Nelson, 44
Weston, Wilson, 44
Wheeler, Moses, 16
Whitefield, George, 27, *28*
Williams Typewriter Co., 59
Wolcott, Oliver, 40
Woodbury, John R., 47
Wooster, David, 29, *30*, 31, 33
Wooster, Edward, 13-14, 15-16
Wooster, Marchant, 34
Wooster, Peter, 29-30
Wooster, Silvester, 31, 33
Wooster, William B., *46*
Wooster family homestead, *31*
World War I, 58, 62-63, *65*
World War II, 66-67

Y
Young Men's Savings Bank and Building Association, 47

Z
Ziomek, Anthony, 70